A long time ago in a galaxy far,
far away....

COLOR SEPARATOR
HAROLD MacKINNON

LETTERER
STEVE DUTRO

EDITOR
DAVID LAND

COVER ART
MIKE MAYHEW

BACK COVER ART
HUGH FLEMING

COLLECTION EDITOR: **MARK D. BEAZLEY**
ASSOCIATE EDITOR: **SARAH BRUNSTAD**
ASSOCIATE MANAGER, DIGITAL ASSETS: **JOE HOCHSTEIN**
ASSOCIATE MANAGING EDITOR: **ALEX STARBUCK**
EDITOR, SPECIAL PROJECTS: **JENNIFER GRÜNWALD**
VP, PRODUCTION & SPECIAL PROJECTS: **JEFF YOUNGQUIST**

SVP PRINT, SALES & MARKETING: **DAVID GABRIEL**
EDITOR IN CHIEF: **AXEL ALONSO**
CHIEF CREATIVE OFFICER: **JOE QUESADA**
PUBLISHER: **DAN BUCKLEY**
EXECUTIVE PRODUCER: **ALAN FINE**

Special Thanks to FRANK PARISI & LUCASFILM; JEPH YORK AND MIKE HANSEN

STAR WARS: EPISODE I - THE PHANTOM MENACE. Contains material originally published in magazine form as STAR WARS: EPISODE I — THE PHANTOM MENACE #1-4. First printing 2016. ISBN# 978-1-302-90074-8. Publis by MARVEL WORLDWIDE, INC., a subsidiary of MARVEL ENTERTAINMENT, LLC. OFFICE OF PUBLICATION: 135 West 50th Street, New York, NY 10020. **Printed in the U.S.A**. ALAN FINE, President, Marvel Entertainm DAN BUCKLEY, President, TV, Publishing & Brand Management; JOE QUESADA, Chief Creative Officer; TOM BREVOORT, SVP of Publishing; DAVID BOGART, SVP of Business Affairs & Operations, Publishing & Partners C.B. CEBULSKI, VP of Brand Management & Development, Asia; DAVID GABRIEL, SVP of Sales & Marketing, Publishing; JEFF YOUNGQUIST, VP of Production & Special Projects; DAN CARR, Executive Director of Publis Technology; ALEX MORALES, Director of Publishing Operations; SUSAN CRESPI, Production Manager; STAN LEE, Chairman Emeritus. For information regarding advertising in Marvel Comics or on Marvel.com, please contac DeBellis, Integrated Sales Manager, at vdebellis@marvel.com. For Marvel subscription inquiries, please call 888-511-5480. **Manufactured between 3/11/2016 and 4/25/2016 by R.R. DONNELLEY, INC., SALEM, VA, U**

10 9 8 7 6 5 4 3 2 1

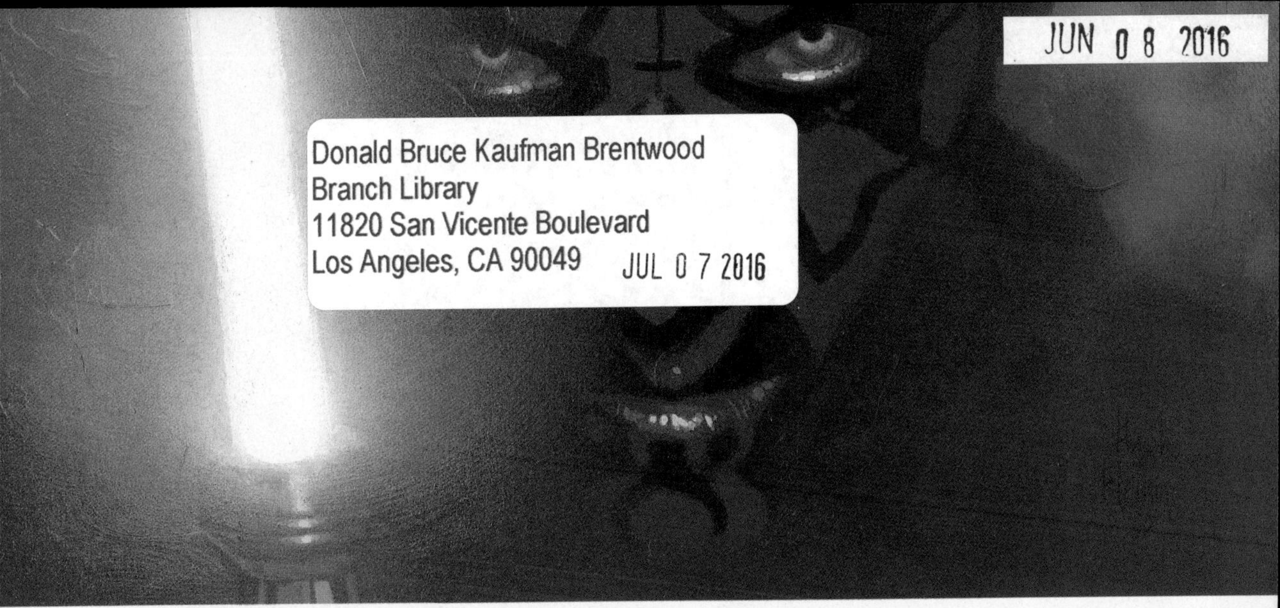

STAR WARS®

THE PHANTOM MENACE

STORY
GEORGE LUCAS

SCRIPT
HENRY GILROY

PENCILER
RODOLFO DAMAGGIO

INKER
AL WILLIAMSON

COLORIST
DAVE NESTELLE

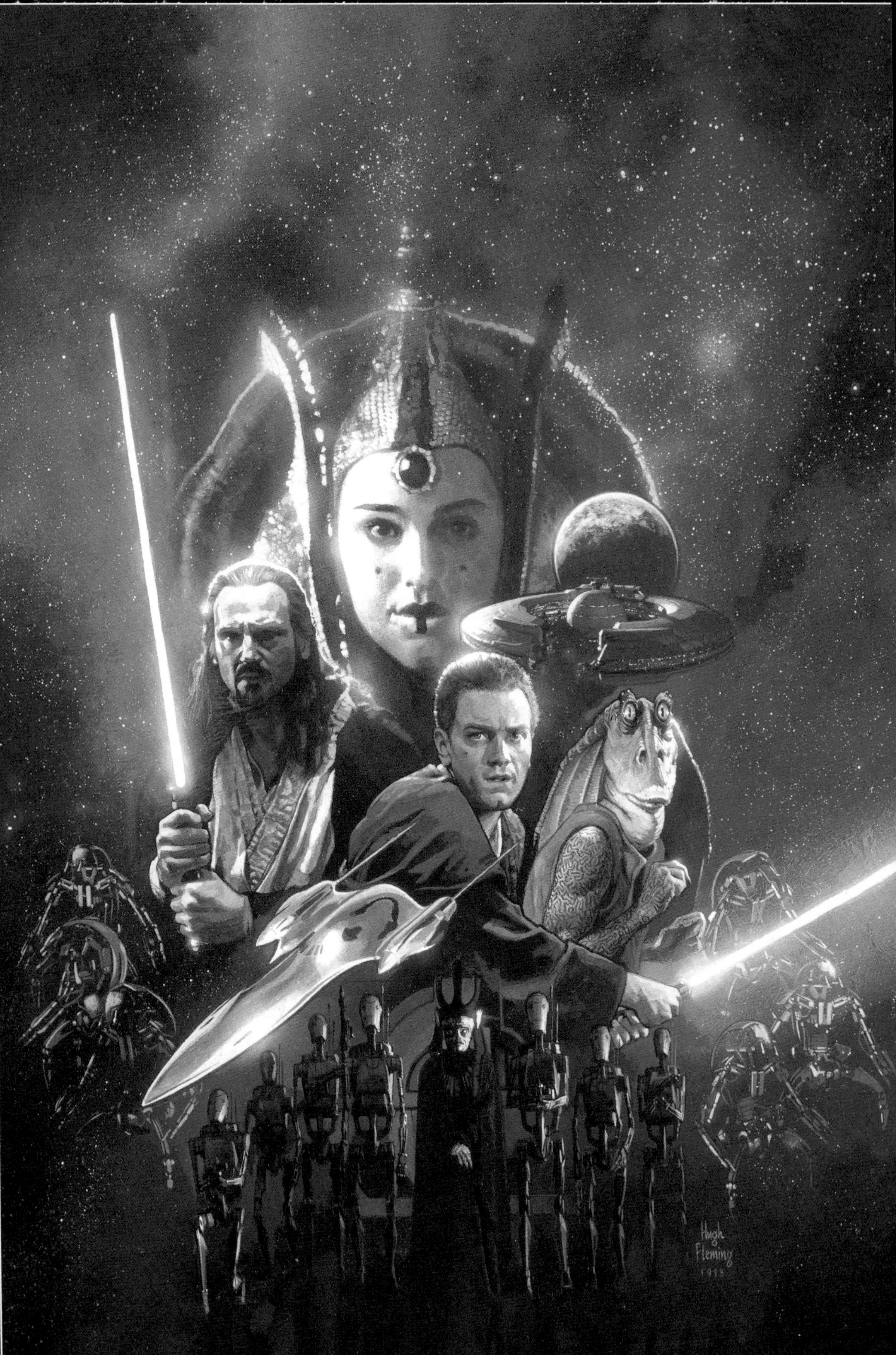
Hugh Fleming

THE PHANTOM MENACE #1

Episode I
THE PHANTOM MENACE

Turmoil has engulfed the Galactic Republic. The taxation of trade routes to outlying star systems is in dispute.

Hoping to resolve the matter with a blockade of deadly battleships, the greedy Trade Federation has stopped all shipping to the small planet of Naboo.

While the Congress of the Republic endlessly debates the alarming chain of events, the Supreme Chancellor has secretly dispatched two Jedi Knights, the guardians of peace and justice in the galaxy, to settle the conflict....

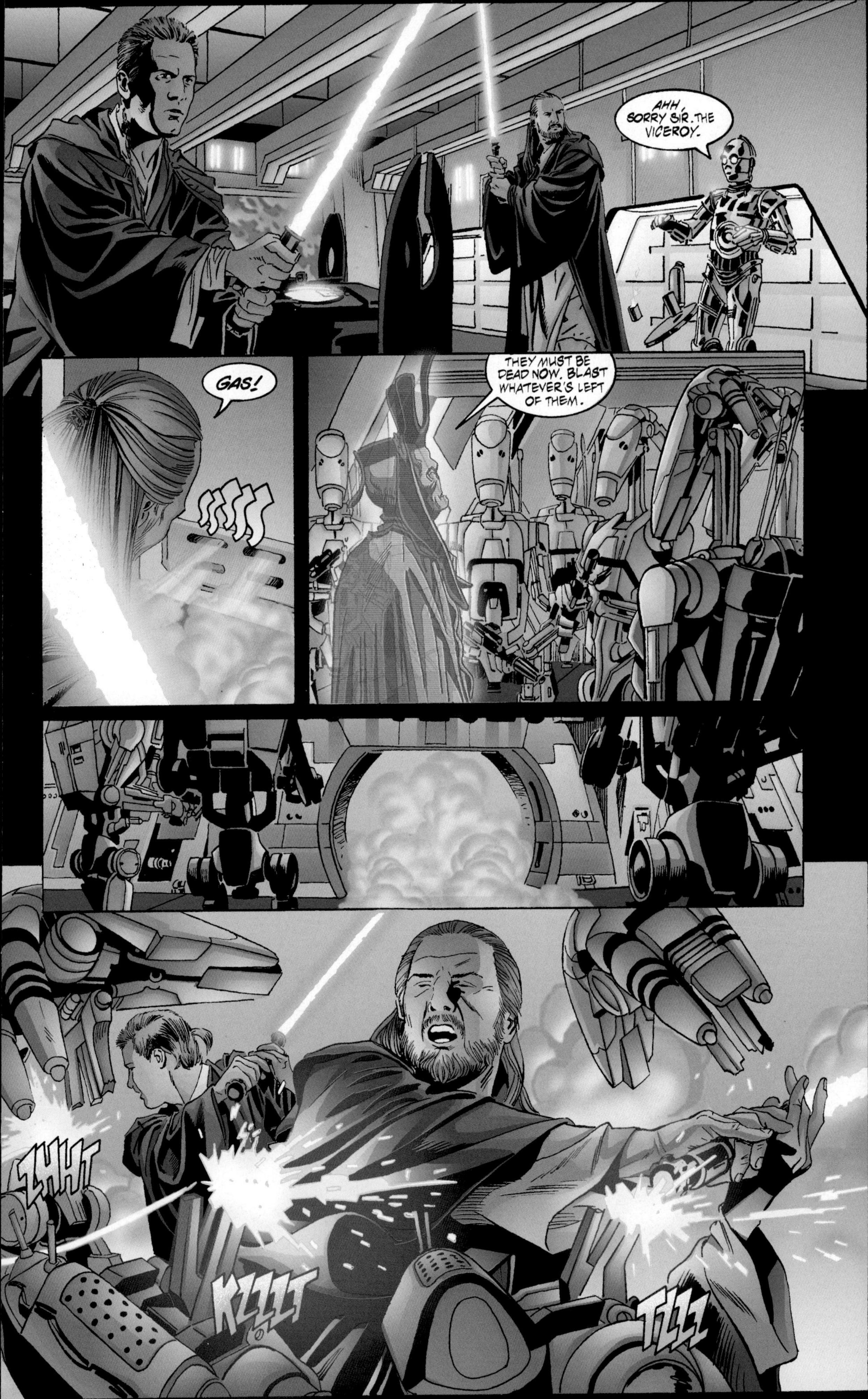
AHH, SORRY SIR. THE VICEROY.
GAS!
THEY MUST BE DEAD NOW. BLAST WHATEVER'S LEFT OF THEM.
ZHHT
KZZZT
TZZZ

QUICKLY, THE ASTROMECH DROIDS WORK TO REPAIR THE DAMAGED VESSEL...

...AND WITH ONE FINAL WELD THE DEFLECTOR SHIELD BECOMES FUNCTIONAL, ALLOWING THE SHIP TO ESCAPE.

YOU SAYEA DUS.

THERE'S NOT ENOUGH POWER TO GET US TO CORUSCANT... THE HYPERDRIVE IS LEAKING.

WE'LL HAVE TO LAND SOMEWHERE TO REFUEL AND REPAIR THE SHIP.

HERE, MASTER. TATOOINE. IT'S SMALL, OUT OF THE WAY, POOR... THE TRADE FEDERATION HAS NO PRESENCE THERE.

IT'S CONTROLLED BY HUTTS.

THE HUTTS? THE HUTTS ARE GANGSTERS! IF THEY DISCOVERED HER...

...IT WOULD BE NO DIFFERENT THAN IF WE LANDED ON A SYSTEM CONTROLLED BY THE FEDERATION...

...EXCEPT THE HUTTS AREN'T LOOKING FOR HER, WHICH GIVES US THE ADVANTAGE.

AN EXTREMELY WELL-PUT-TOGETHER LITTLE DROID.

WITHOUT A DOUBT, IT SAVED THE SHIP AS WELL AS OUR LIVES.

IT IS TO BE COMMENDED. WHAT IS ITS NUMBER?

R2-D2, YOUR HIGHNESS.

WHOOT EEEET OOOO!

THANK YOU, ARTOO-DETOO. YOU HAVE PROVEN TO BE VERY LOYAL.

PADMÉ! CLEAN THIS DROID UP THE BEST YOU CAN. IT DESERVES OUR GRATITUDE.

YOUR HIGHNESS, WE ARE HEADING FOR A REMOTE PLANET CALLED TATOOINE.

YOUR HIGHNESS, TATOOINE IS VERY DANGEROUS. I DO NOT AGREE WITH THE JEDI ON THIS.

YOU MUST TRUST MY JUDGEMENT, YOUR HIGHNESS.

ON THE JEDI'S RECOMMENDATION, THE QUEEN ORDERS HER SHIP TO SET COURSE FOR THE PLANET OF TATOOINE.

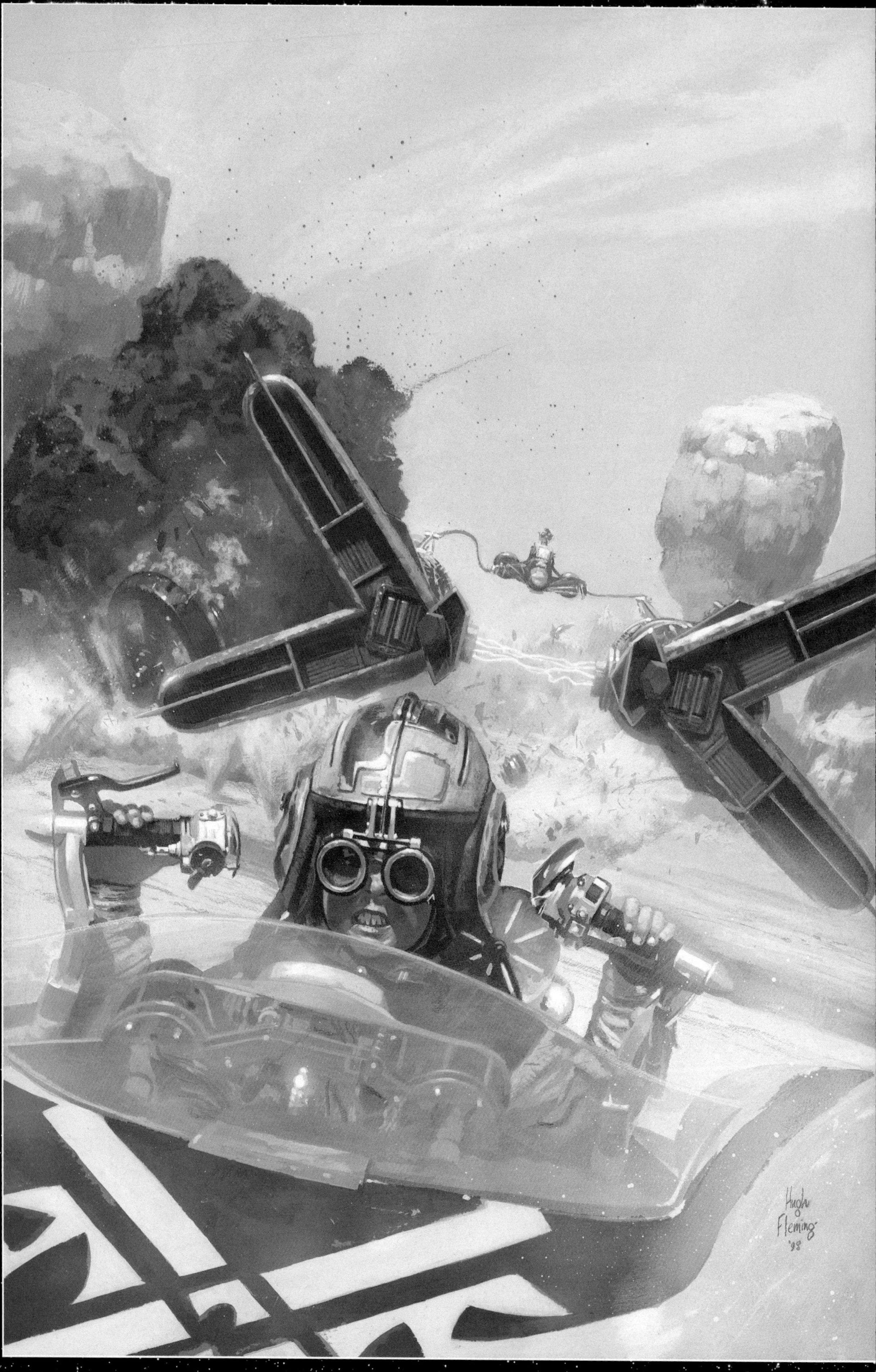
Hugh Fleming '98

THE PHANTOM MENACE #2

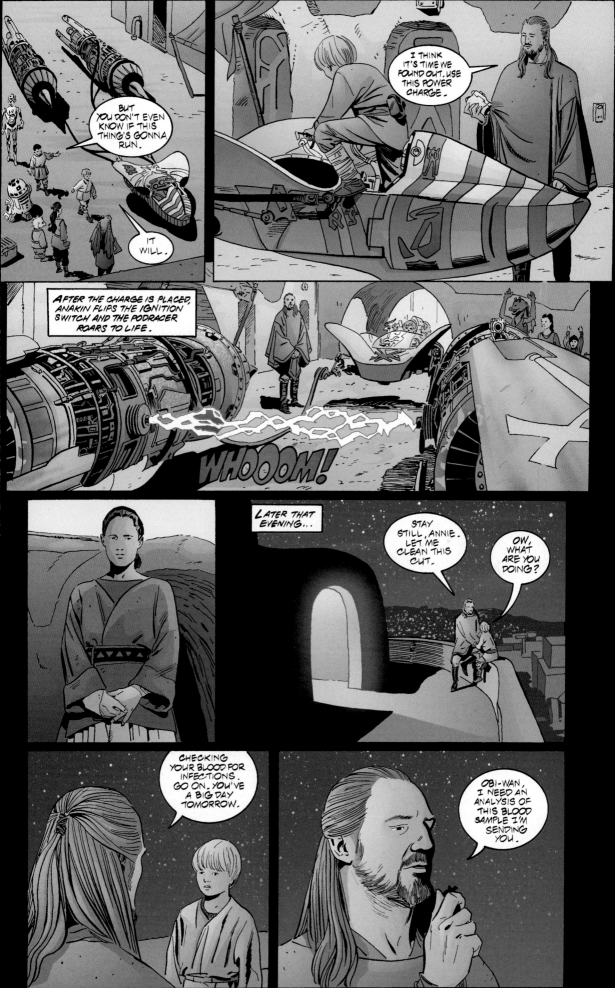

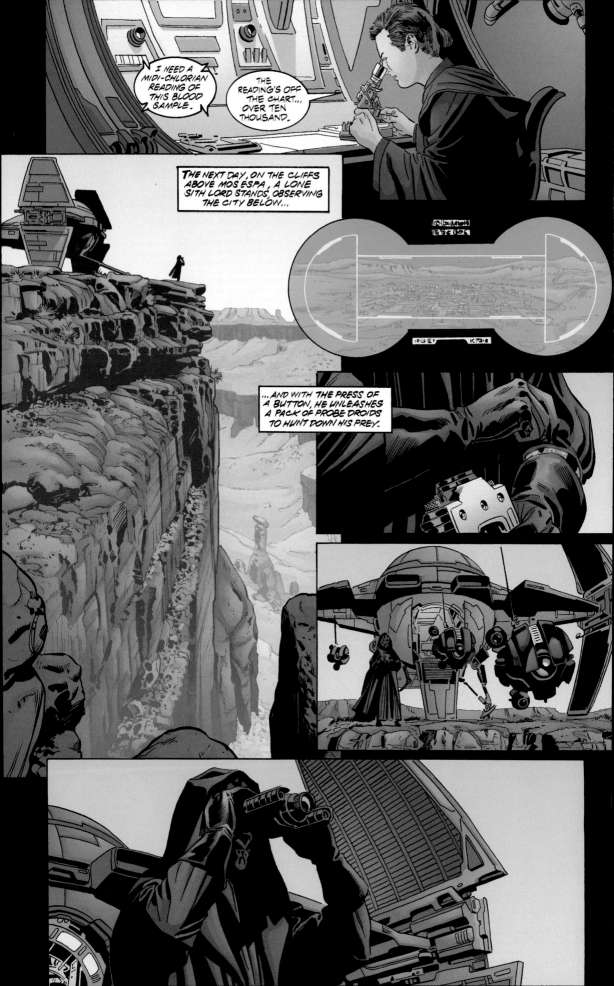

I NEED A MIDI-CHLORIAN READING OF THIS BLOOD SAMPLE.

THE READING'S OFF THE CHART... OVER TEN THOUSAND.

THE NEXT DAY, ON THE CLIFFS ABOVE MOS ESPA, A LONE SITH LORD STANDS, OBSERVING THE CITY BELOW...

...AND WITH THE PRESS OF A BUTTON, HE UNLEASHES A PACK OF PROBE DROIDS TO HUNT DOWN HIS PREY.

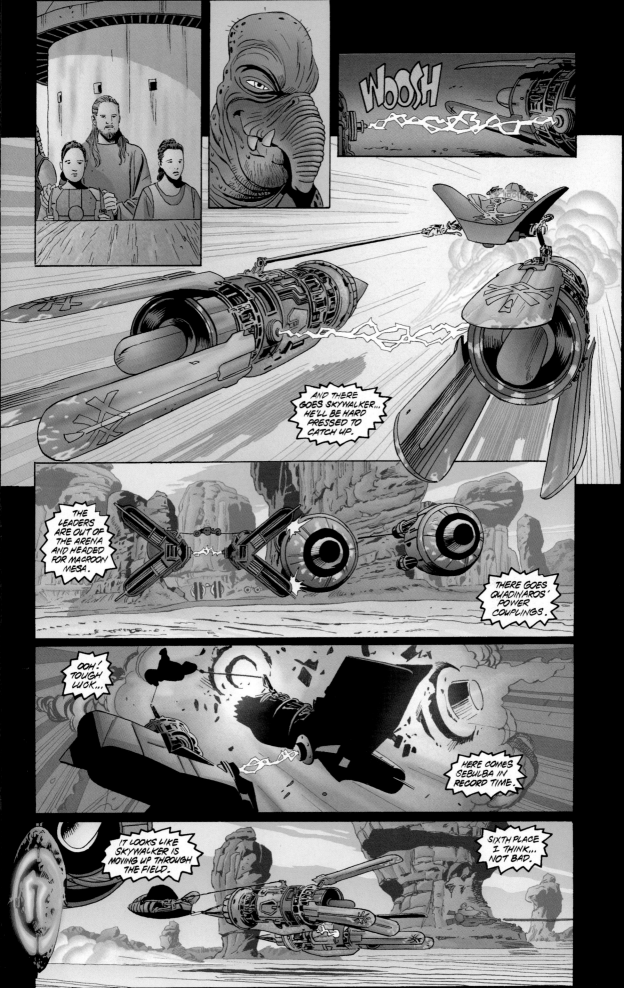

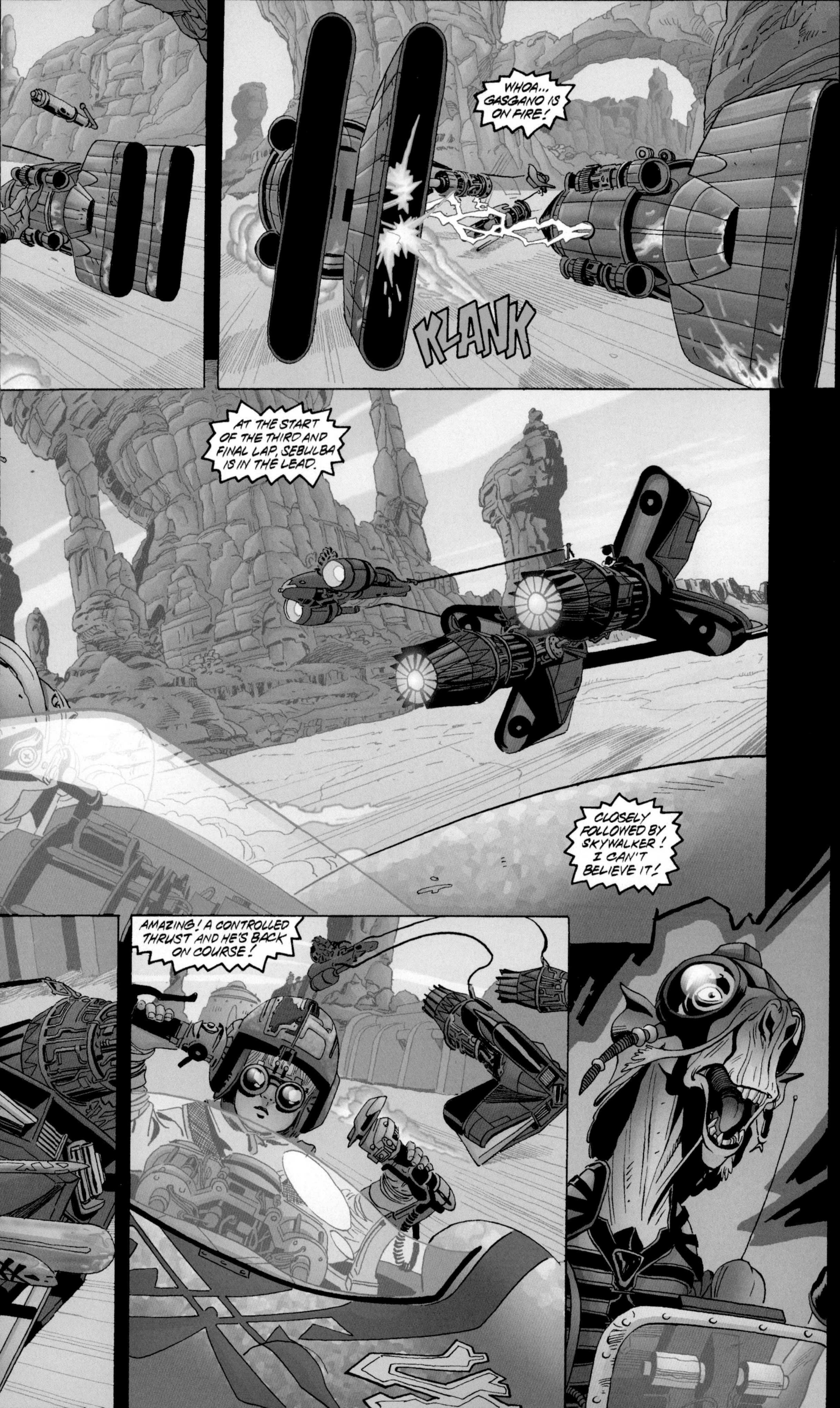
WHOA... GASGANO IS ON FIRE!
KLANK
AT THE START OF THE THIRD AND FINAL LAP, SEBULBA IS IN THE LEAD.
CLOSELY FOLLOWED BY SKYWALKER! I CAN'T BELIEVE IT!
AMAZING! A CONTROLLED THRUST AND HE'S BACK ON COURSE!

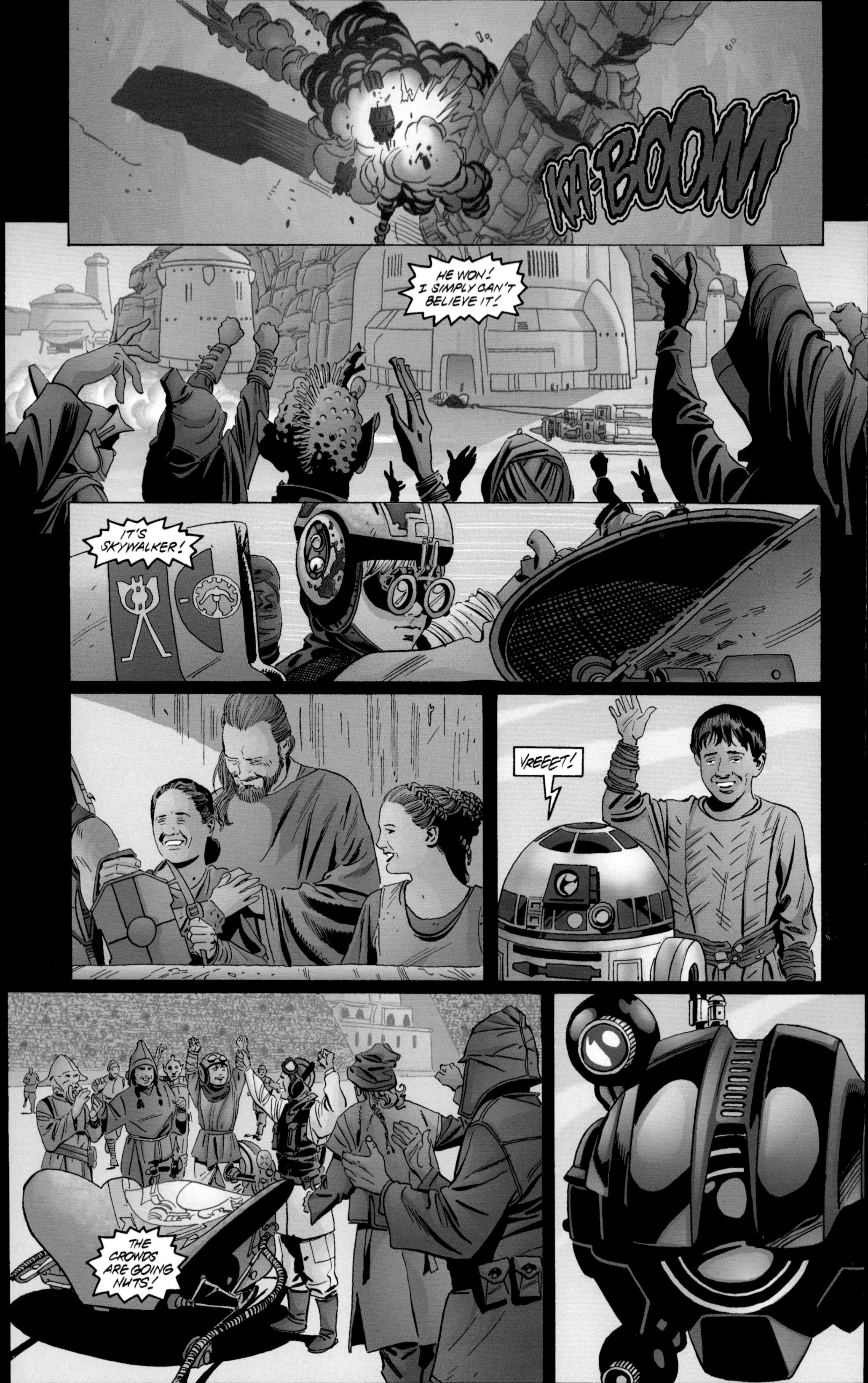
KA-BOOM!
HE WON! I SIMPLY CAN'T BELIEVE IT!
IT'S SKYWALKER!
VREEET!
THE CROWDS ARE GOING NUTS!

THE PHANTOM MENACE #3

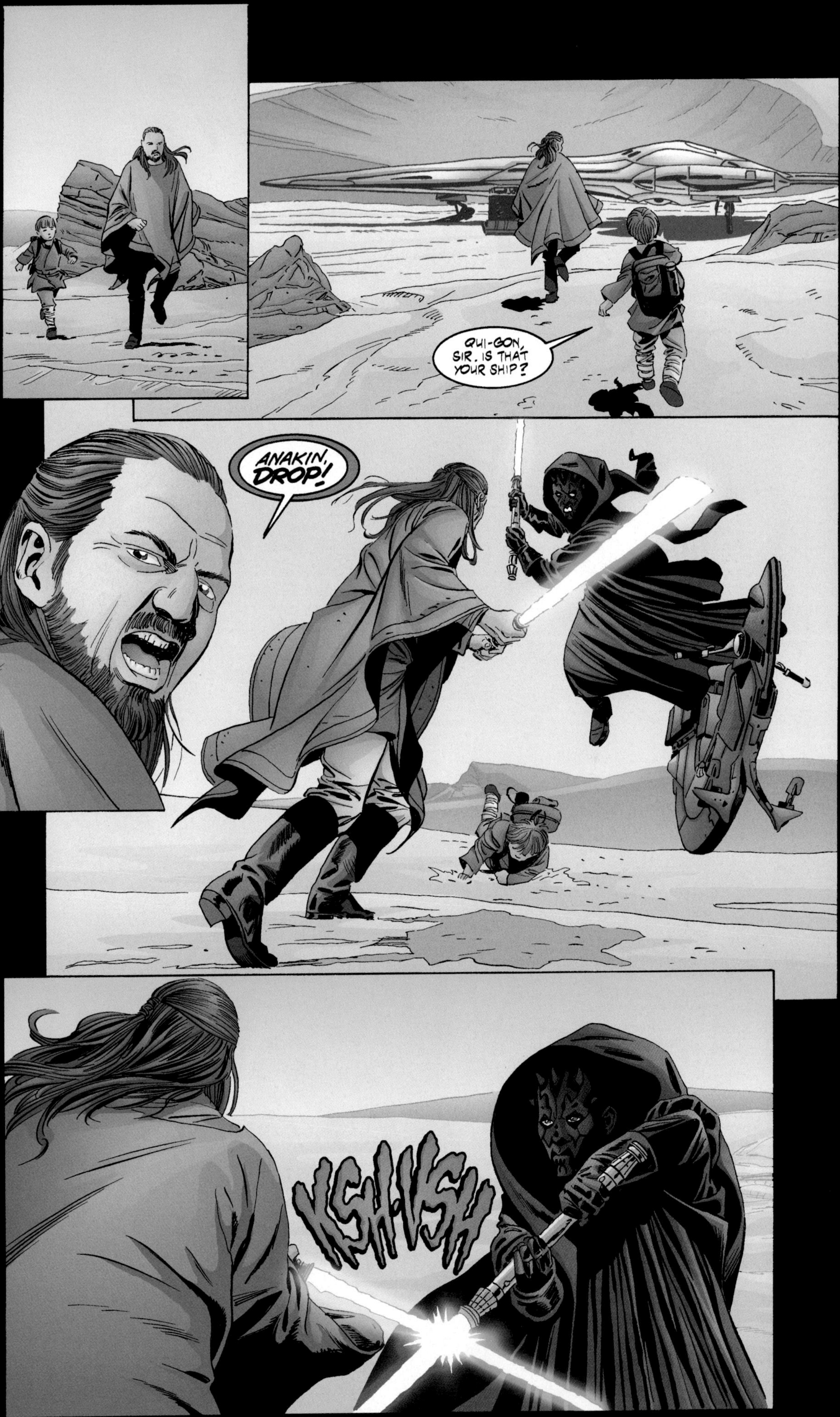
QUI-GON, SIR. IS THAT YOUR SHIP?
ANAKIN, DROP!
KSH-VSH

KSST

THUMP

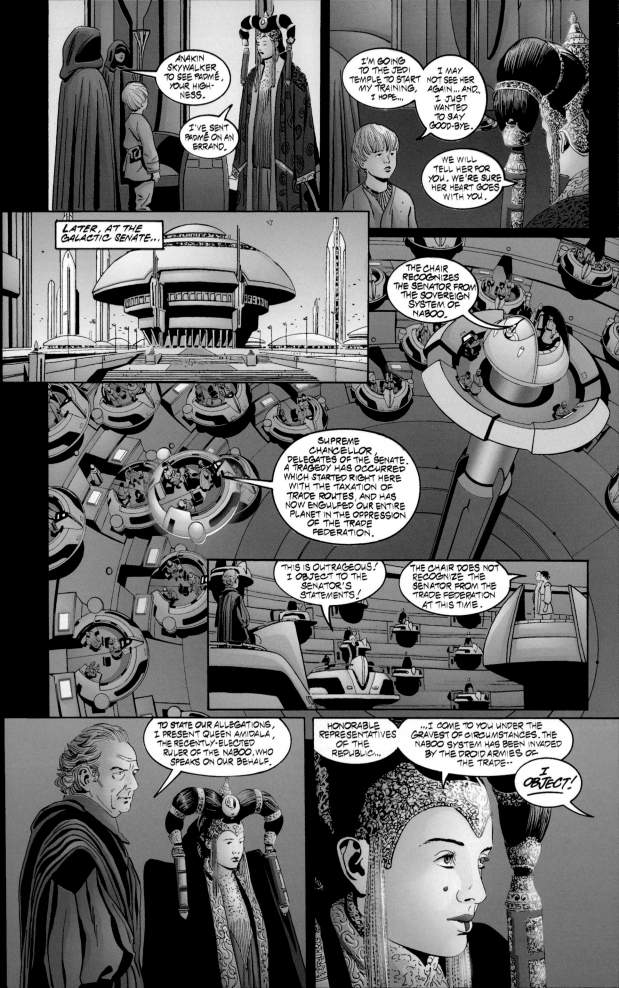

THE PHANTOM MENACE #4

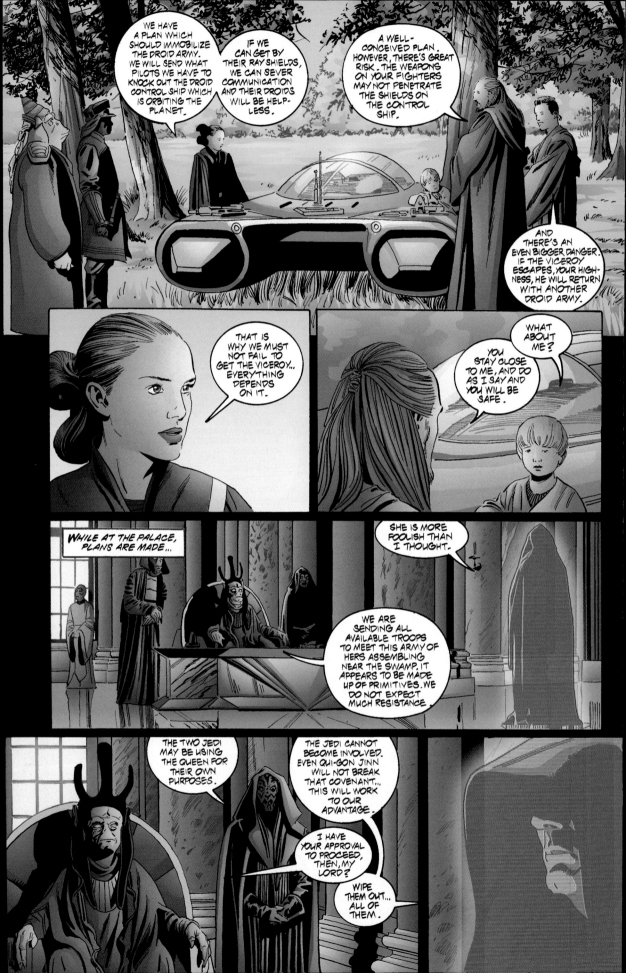

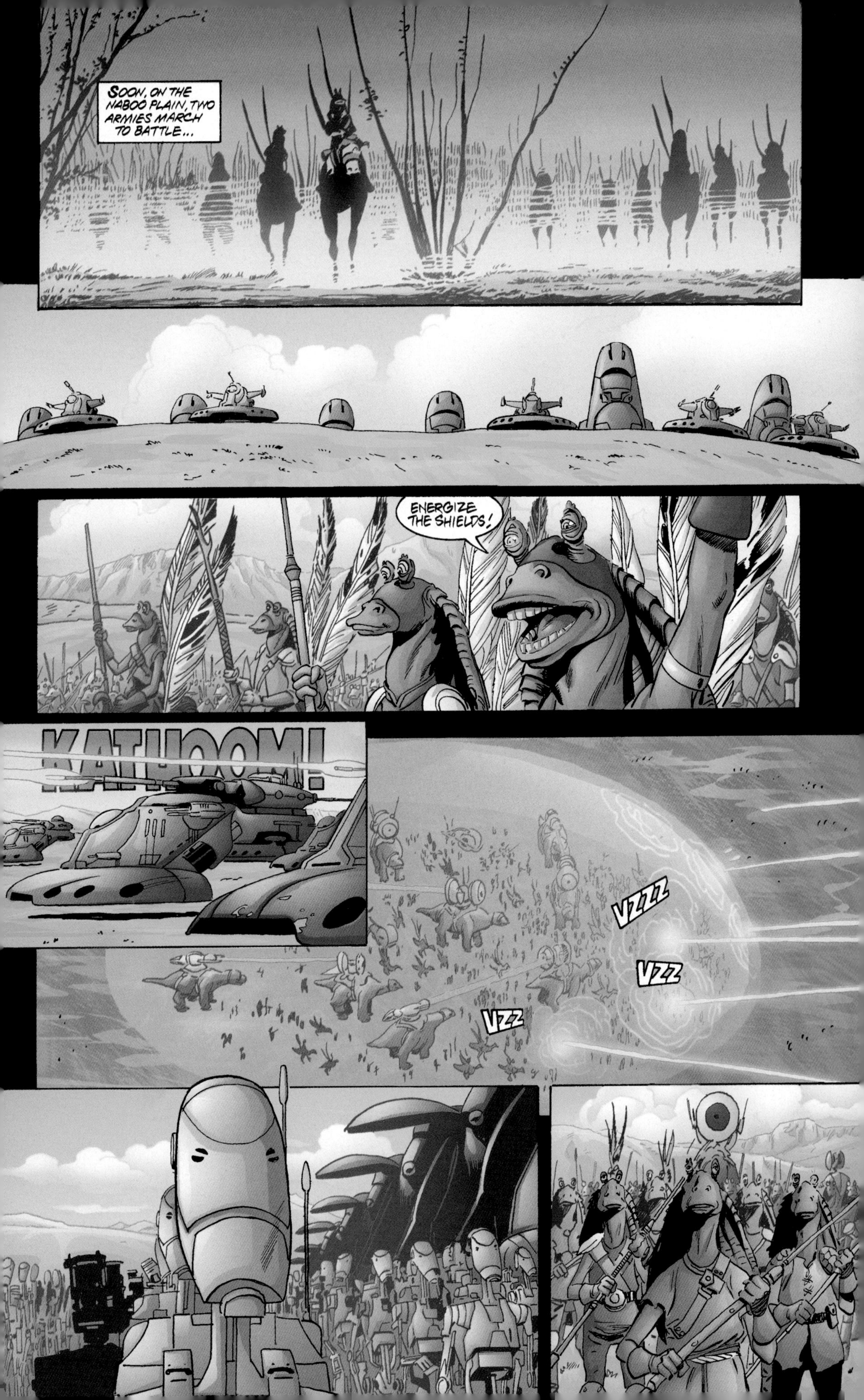

SOON, ON THE NABOO PLAIN, TWO ARMIES MARCH TO BATTLE...
ENERGIZE THE SHIELDS!
KATHOOM!
VZZZZ
VZZ
VZZ

BACK AT THE HANGAR, DESTROYER DROIDS ROLL IN TO ATTACK.

BWEEP!

WE GOTTA DO SOMETHING, ARTOO! OH, NO! PADMÉ'S TRAPPED!

ALL RIGHT, THANKS, ARTOO! GREAT IDEA! I'LL TAKE OVER!

OOPS! WRONG ONE... MAYBE THIS ONE...

PRESSING BUTTONS ON THE SHIP'S CONTROL PANEL, ANAKIN ACTIVATES THE LASERS...

BREEOO!

WIZARDS, THAT'S COOL!

THOOM

SHOOM

...COVERING THE ADVANCEMENT OF THE QUEEN AND HER GUARD.

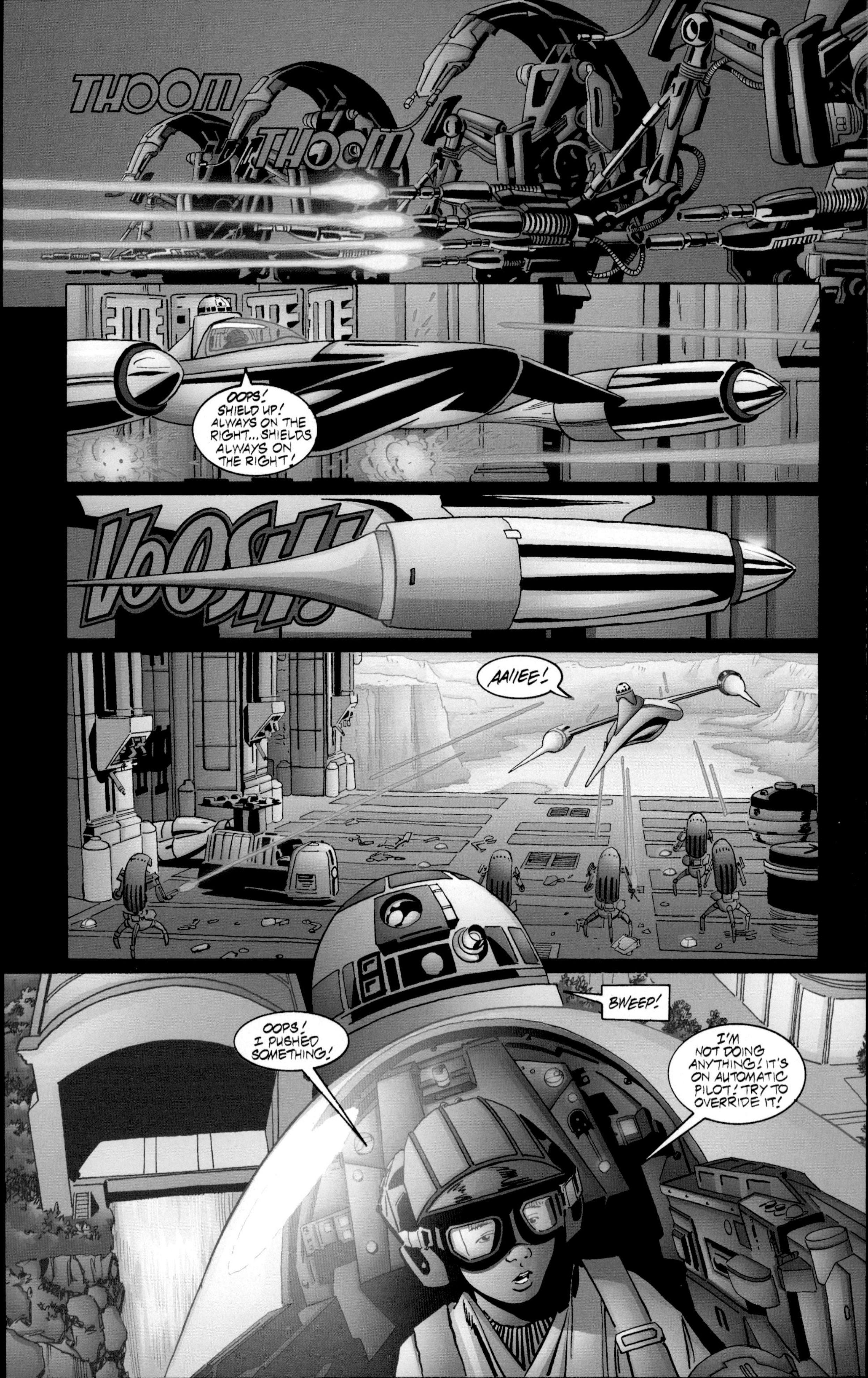
THOOM
THOOM
OOPS! SHIELD UP! ALWAYS ON THE RIGHT... SHIELDS ALWAYS ON THE RIGHT!
VOOSH!
AAIIEE!
BWEEP!
OOPS! I PUSHED SOMETHING!
I'M NOT DOING ANYTHING! IT'S ON AUTOMATIC PILOT! TRY TO OVERRIDE IT!

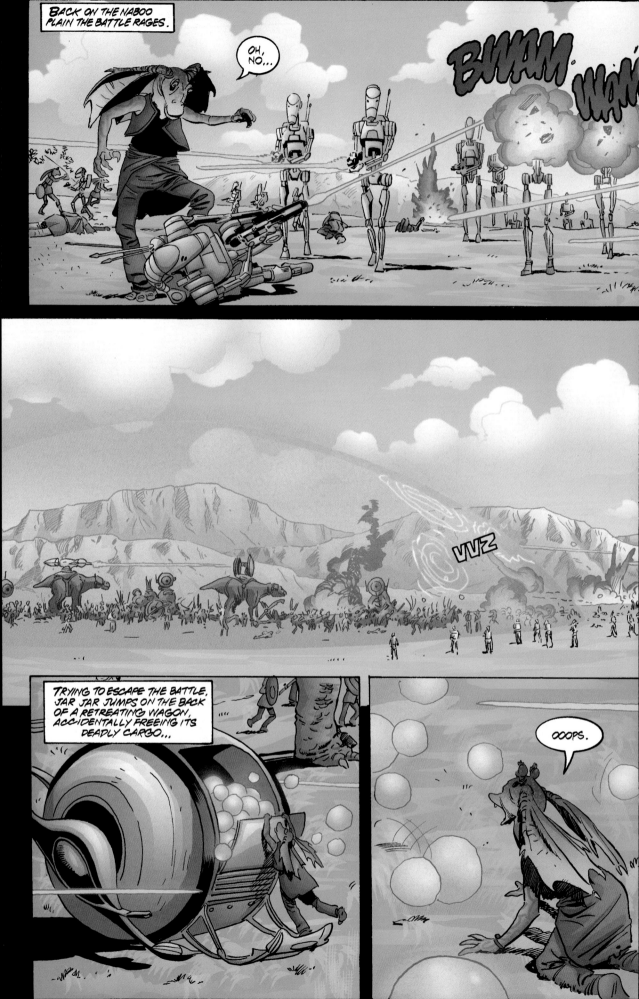

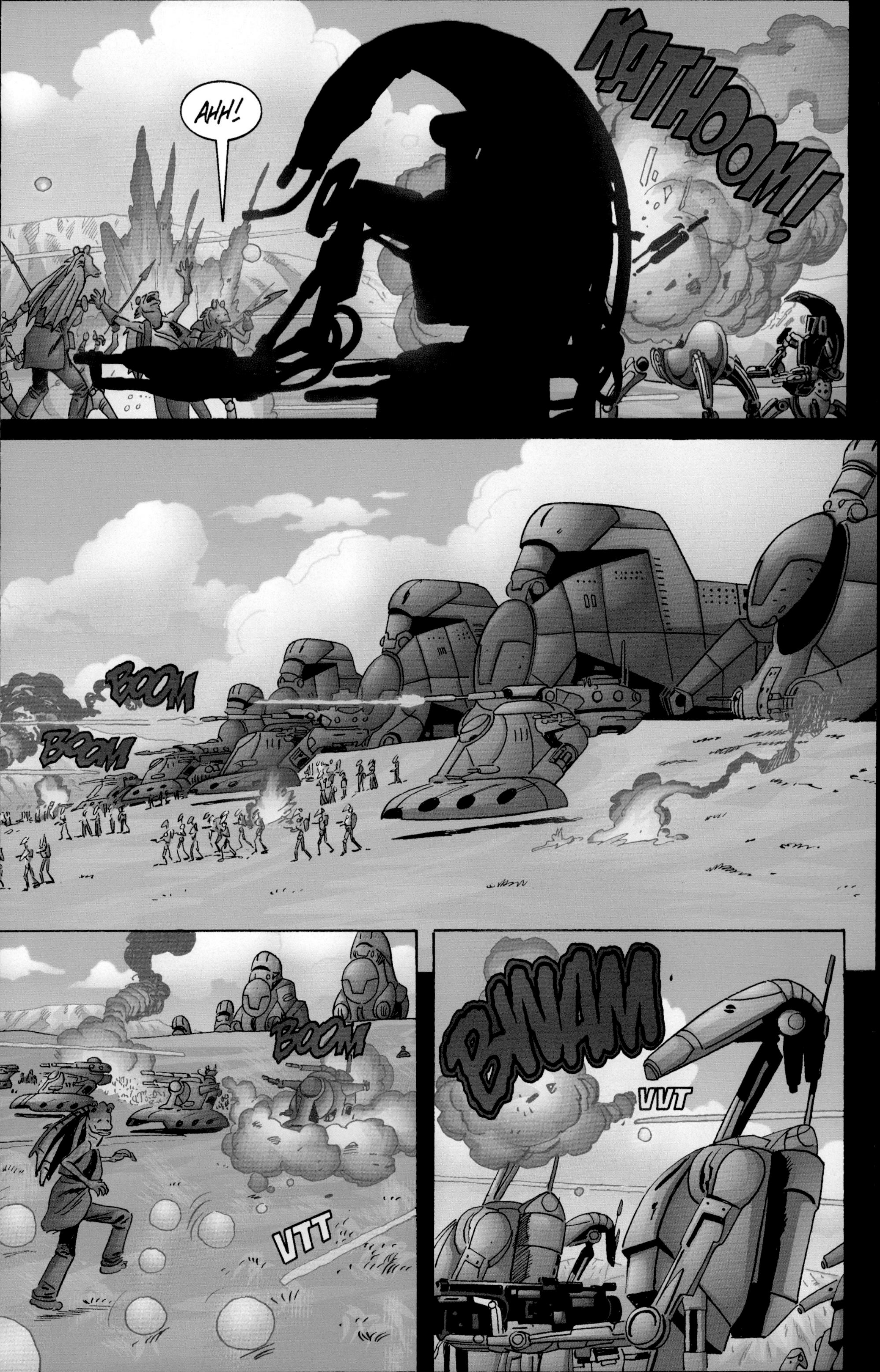
AHH!
KATHOOM!
BOOM
BOOM
BOOM
VTT
BWAM
VVT

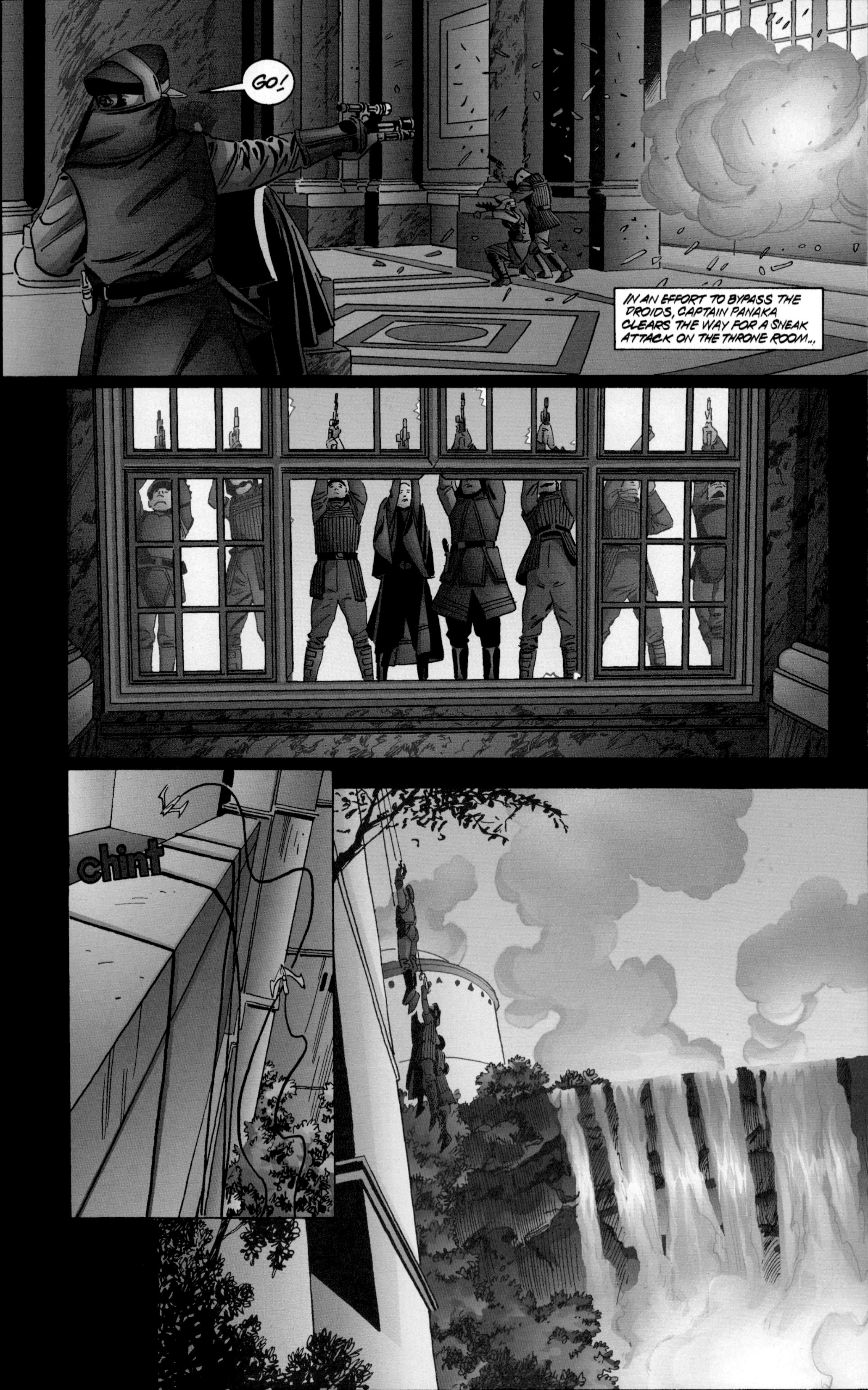
GO!
IN AN EFFORT TO BYPASS THE DROIDS, CAPTAIN PANAKA CLEARS THE WAY FOR A SNEAK ATTACK ON THE THRONE ROOM...
chint

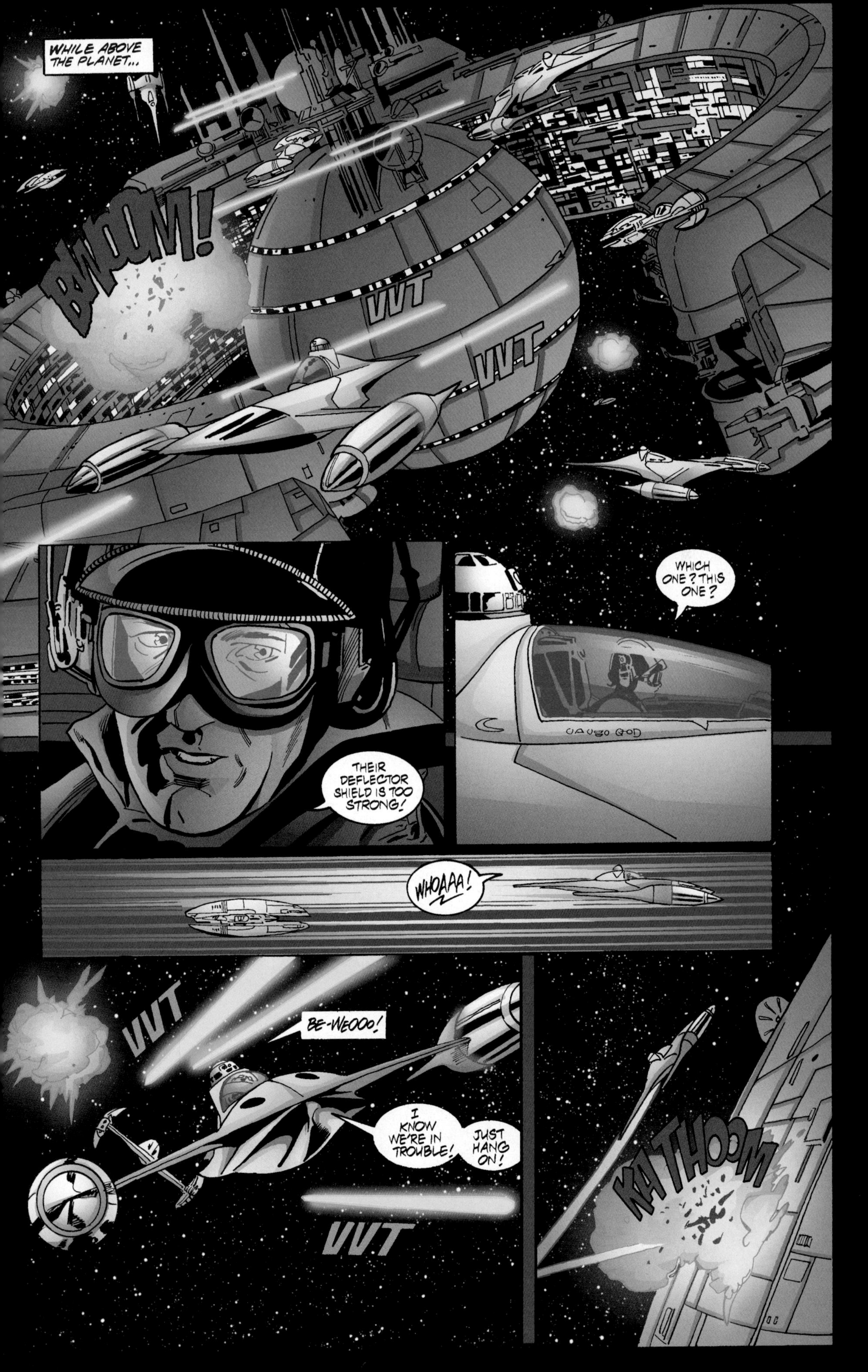
WHILE ABOVE THE PLANET...
BAWOOM!
VVT
VVT
THEIR DEFLECTOR SHIELD IS TOO STRONG!
WHICH ONE? THIS ONE?
WHOAAA!
VVT
BE-WEOOO!
I KNOW WE'RE IN TROUBLE!
JUST HANG ON!
VVT
KA THOOM

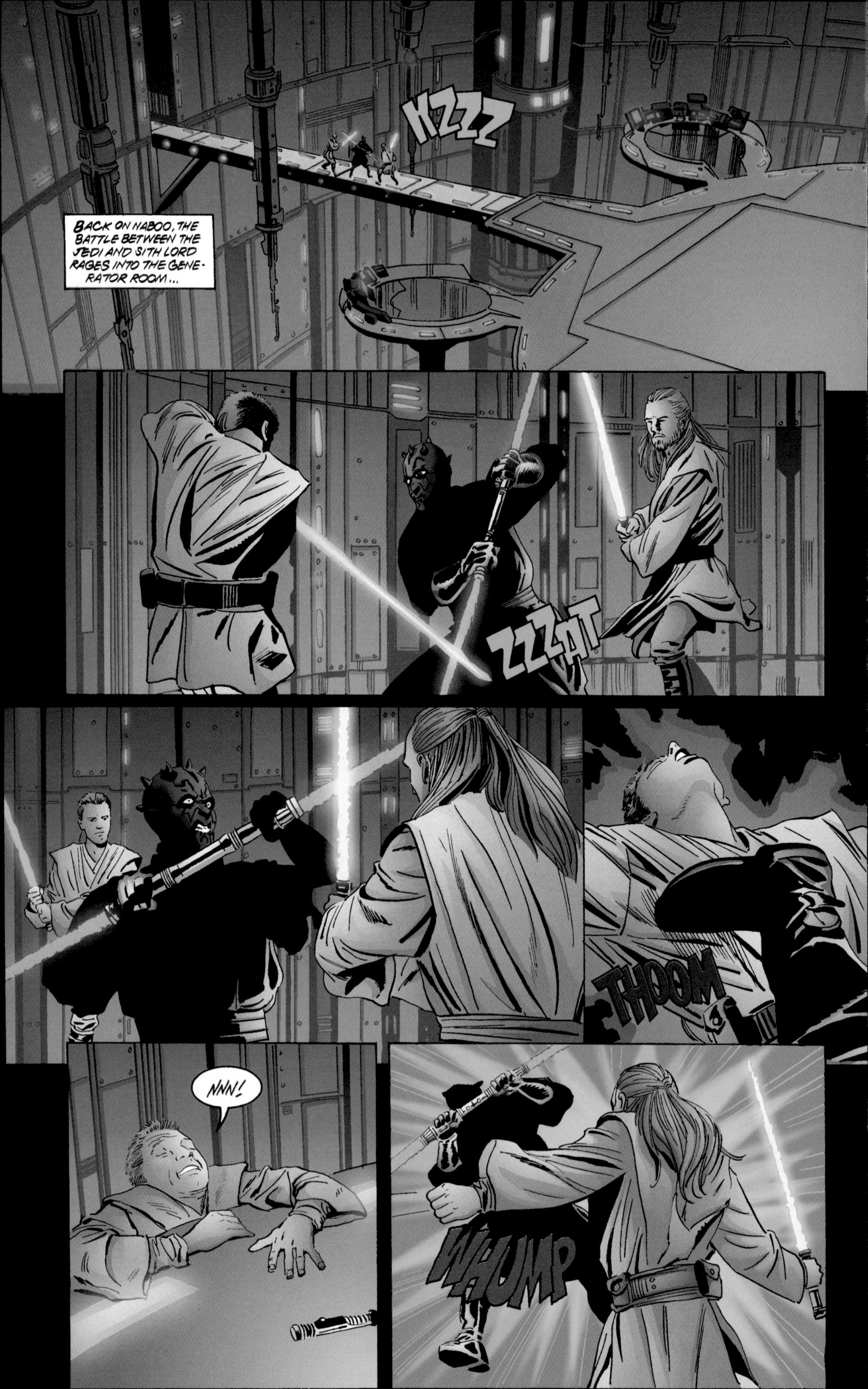
HZZZ
BACK ON NABOO, THE BATTLE BETWEEN THE JEDI AND SITH LORD RAGES INTO THE GENERATOR ROOM...
ZZZAT
THOOM
NNN!
WHUMP

VZZZ

QUI-GON FORCES THE SITH LORD BACK, FURTHER INTO THE GENERATOR ROOM, DANGEROUSLY NEAR THE DEADLY, PULSING CONTAINMENT BEAMS...

BRIEFLY, THE BEAMS CUT THE THREE COMBATANTS OFF FROM ONE ANOTHER, OFFERING A RARE PAUSE IN THE BATTLE.

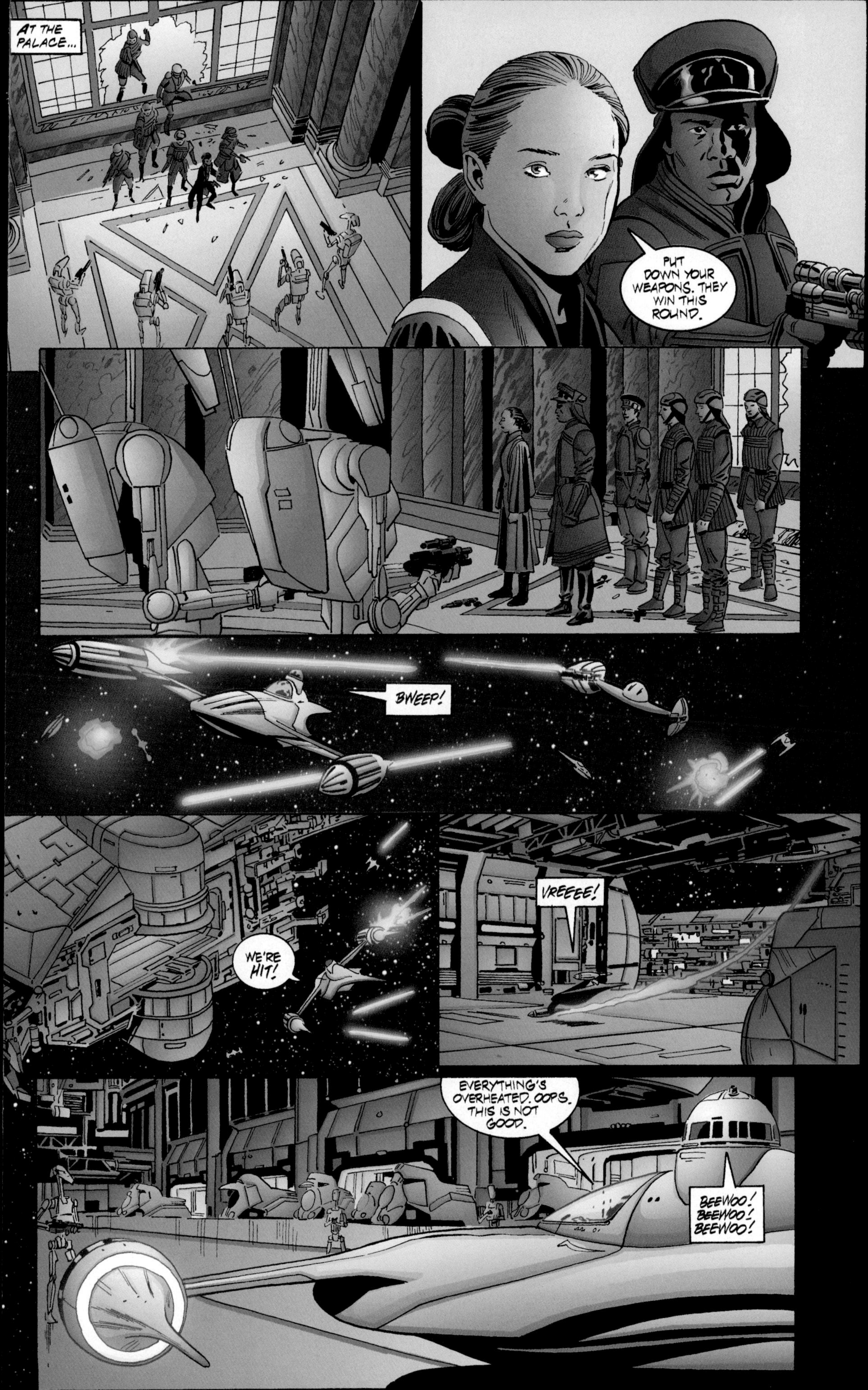
AT THE PALACE...
PUT DOWN YOUR WEAPONS. THEY WIN THIS ROUND.
BWEEP!
WE'RE HIT!
VREEEE!
EVERYTHING'S OVERHEATED. OOPS. THIS IS NOT GOOD.
BEEWOO! BEEWOO! BEEWOO!

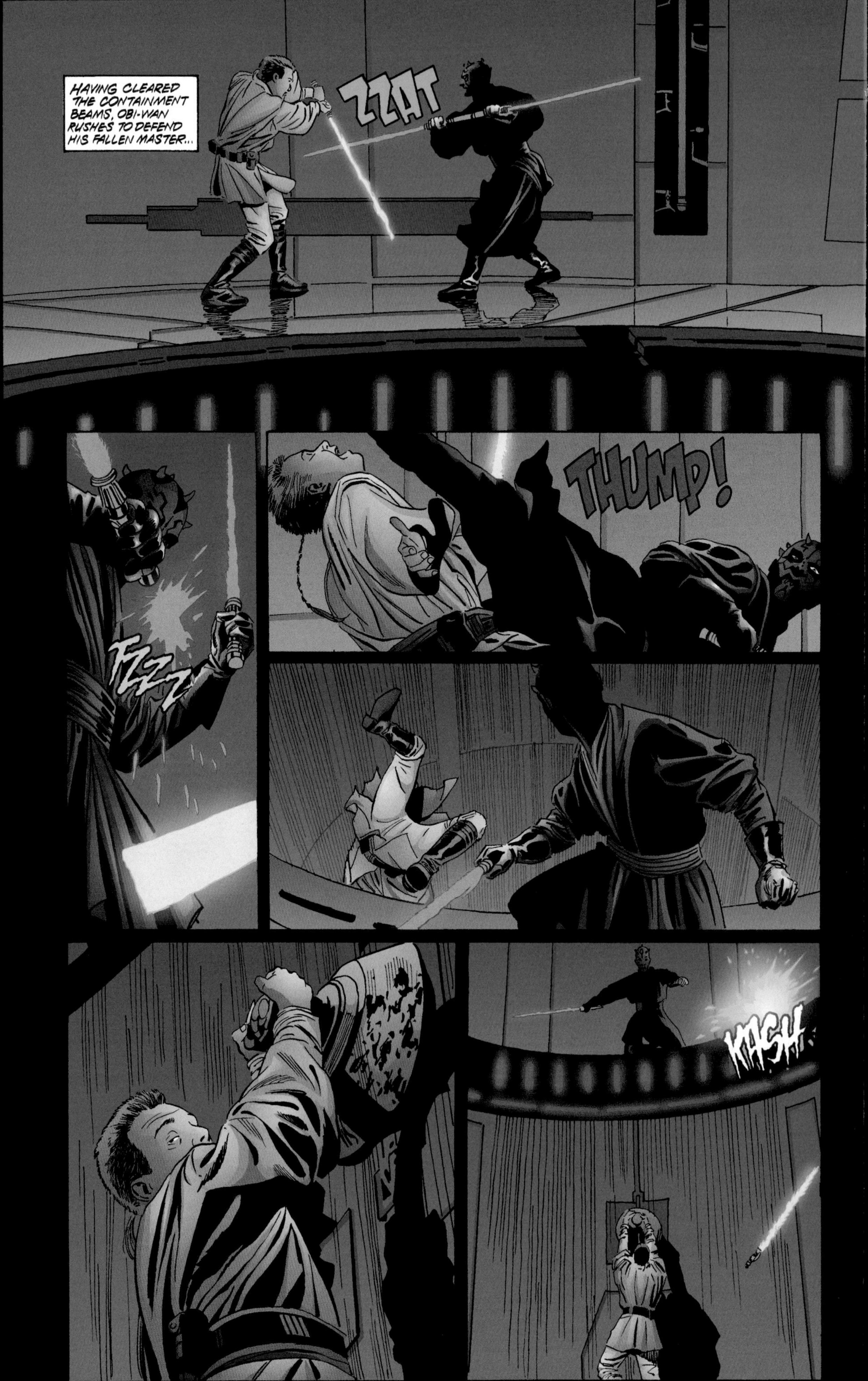
HAVING CLEARED THE CONTAINMENT BEAMS, OBI-WAN RUSHES TO DEFEND HIS FALLEN MASTER...
ZZAT
FZZZ
THUMP!
KASH

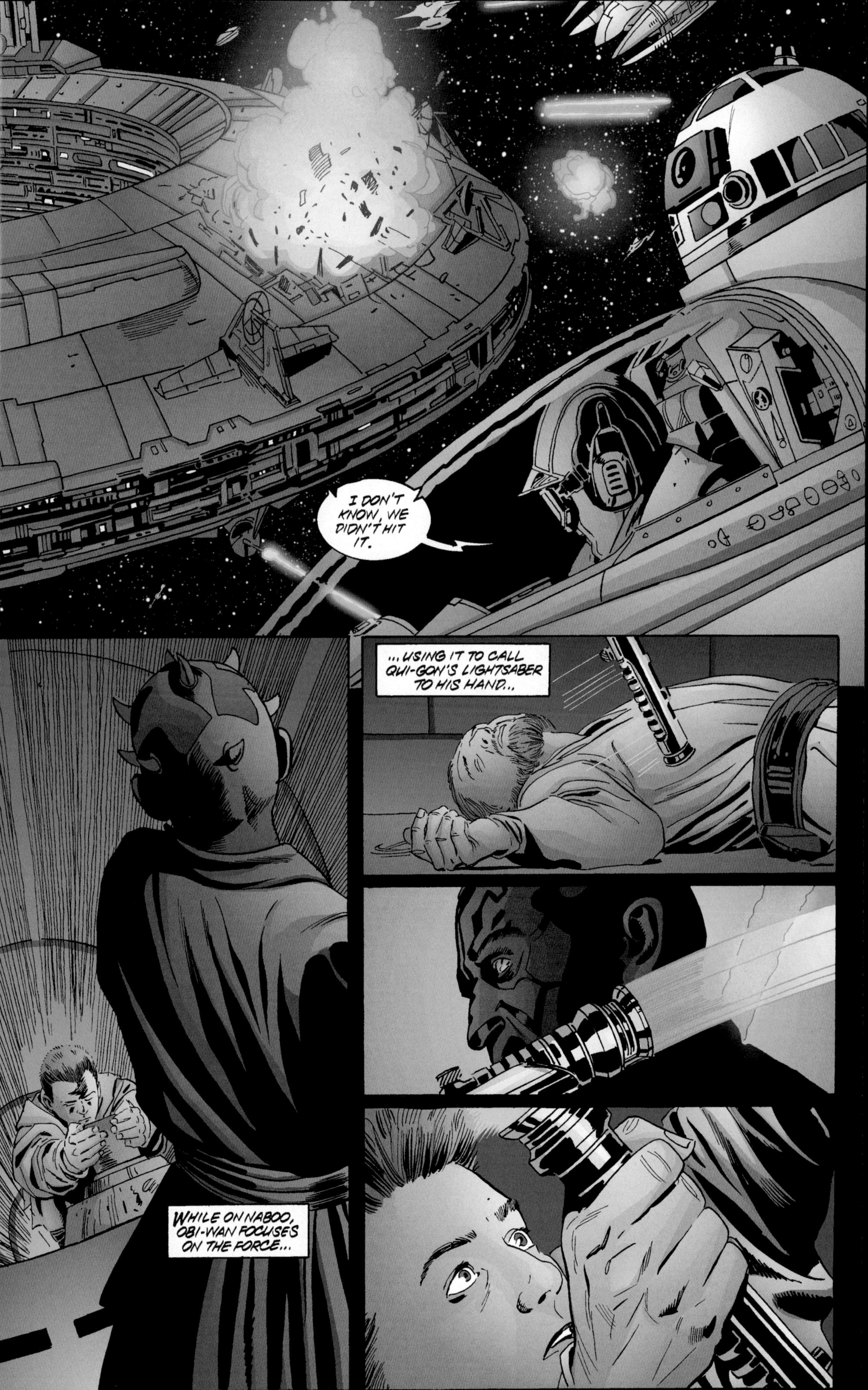
I DON'T KNOW, WE DIDN'T HIT IT.
...USING IT TO CALL QUI-GON'S LIGHTSABER TO HIS HAND...
WHILE ON NABOO, OBI-WAN FOCUSES ON THE FORCE...

FFZZZT

...AND, WITH THE AID OF THE FORCE, OBI-WAN LEAPS FROM THE PIT AND HALVES THE SITH LORD IN ONE SWIFT MOVEMENT...

MASTER! MASTER!

NO!

IT'S TOO LATE... IT'S...

OBI-WAN... PROMISE... PROMISE ME YOU'LL TRAIN THE BOY...

YES, MASTER.

HE IS THE CHOSEN ONE... HE WILL... BRING BALANCE... TRAIN HIM...

WITH THE DESTRUCTION OF THEIR CONTROL SHIP, THE DROIDS ON THE NABOO PLAIN BEGIN TO MALFUNCTION...

BUT MESA DO A NUTIN'.

LATER, NEAR THE PALACE...

VICEROY, YOU ARE GOING BACK TO THE SENATE AND EXPLAIN ALL OF THIS.

I THINK YOU CAN KISS YOUR TRADE FRANCHISE GOODBYE.

CONGRATULATIONS ON YOUR ELECTION, CHANCELLOR.

YOUR BOLDNESS HAS SAVED OUR PEOPLE, YOUR MAJESTY. IT IS YOU WHO SHOULD BE CONGRATULATED. TOGETHER WE SHALL BRING PEACE AND PROSPERITY TO THE REPUBLIC.

LATER, JEDI AND DIGNITARIES GATHER TO BID FAREWELL TO THE FALLEN QUI-GON JINN.

WHAT WILL HAPPEN TO ME NOW?

THE COUNCIL HAS GRANTED ME PERMISSION TO TRAIN YOU.

THERE IS NO DOUBT. THE MYSTERIOUS WARRIOR IS A SITH.

ALWAYS TWO THERE ARE... NO MORE... NO LESS. A MASTER AND HIS APPRENTICE.

BUT WHICH ONE WAS DESTROYED, THE MASTER OR THE APPRENTICE?

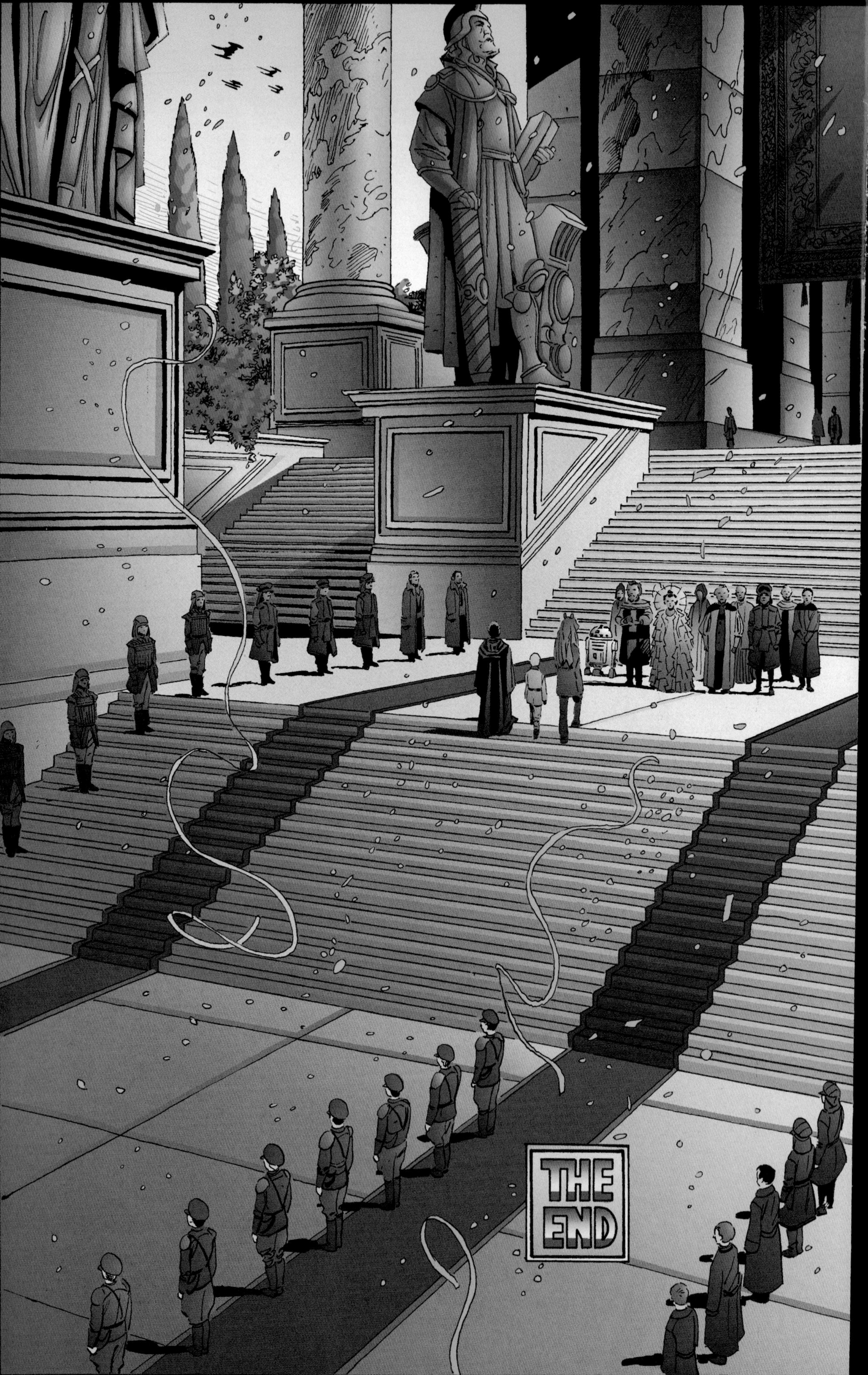
THE END

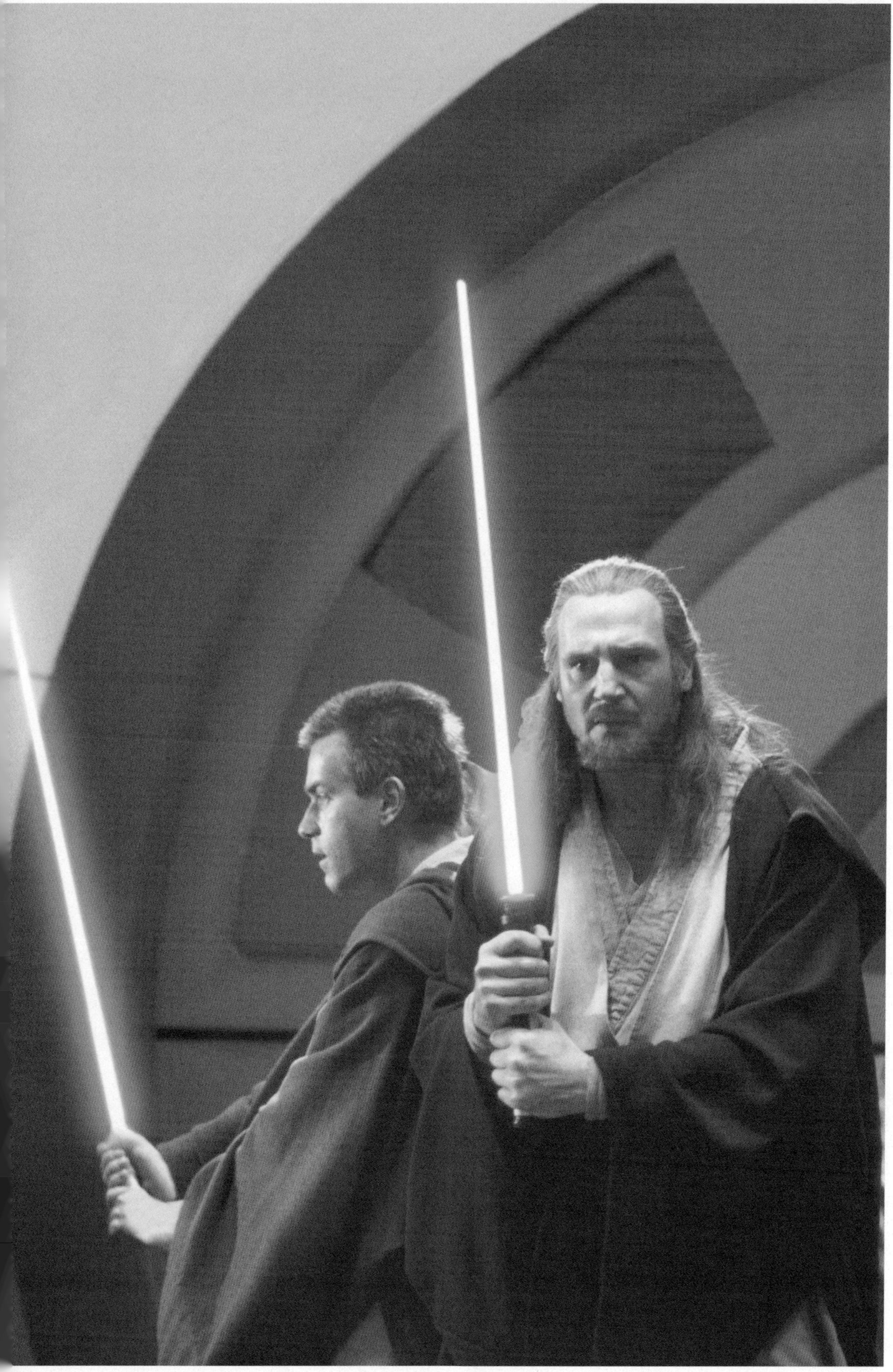

Star Wars: Episode I *The Phantom Menace #1* Photo Variant cover

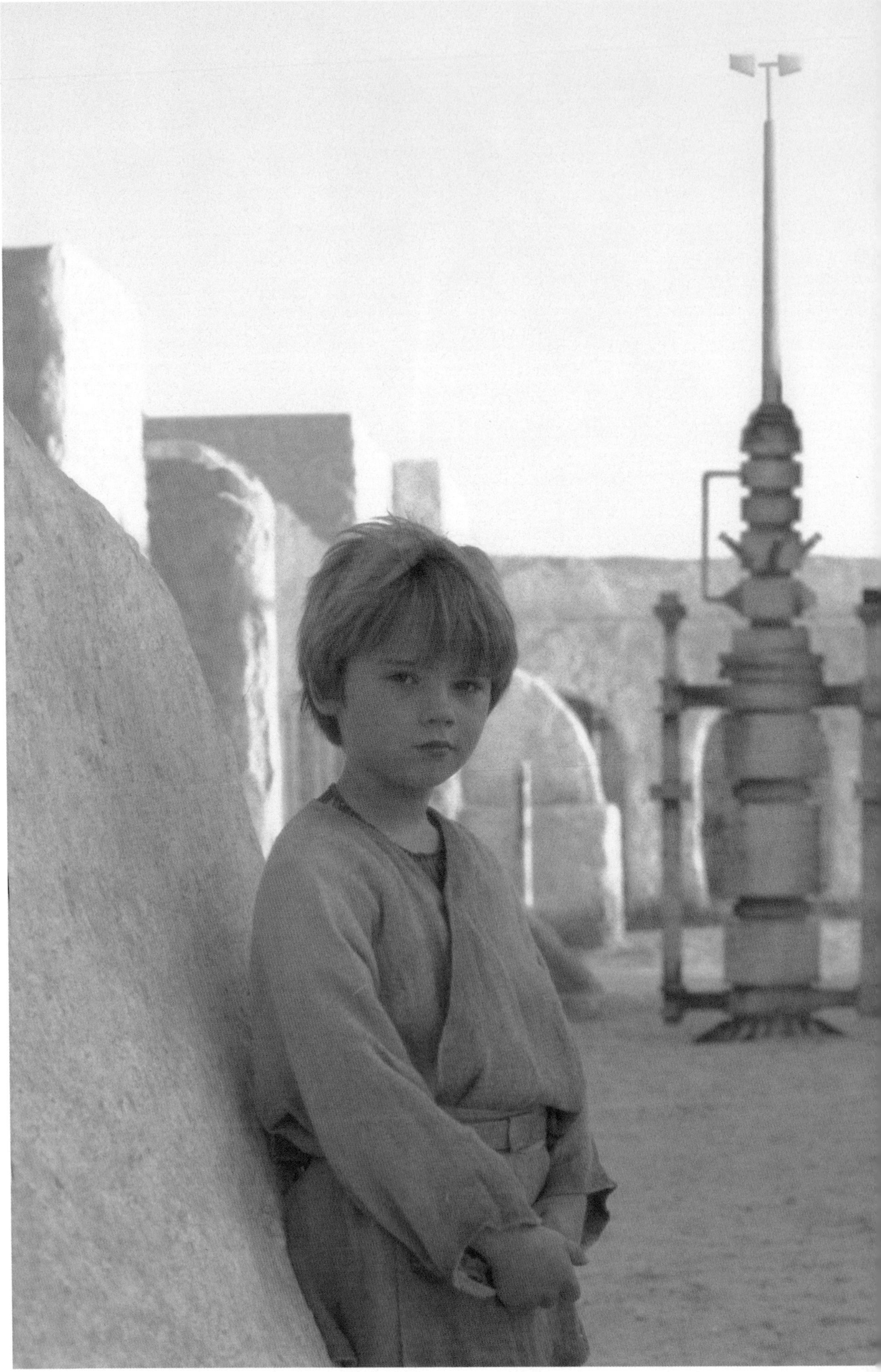

Star Wars: Episode I *The Phantom Menace #2* Photo Variant cover

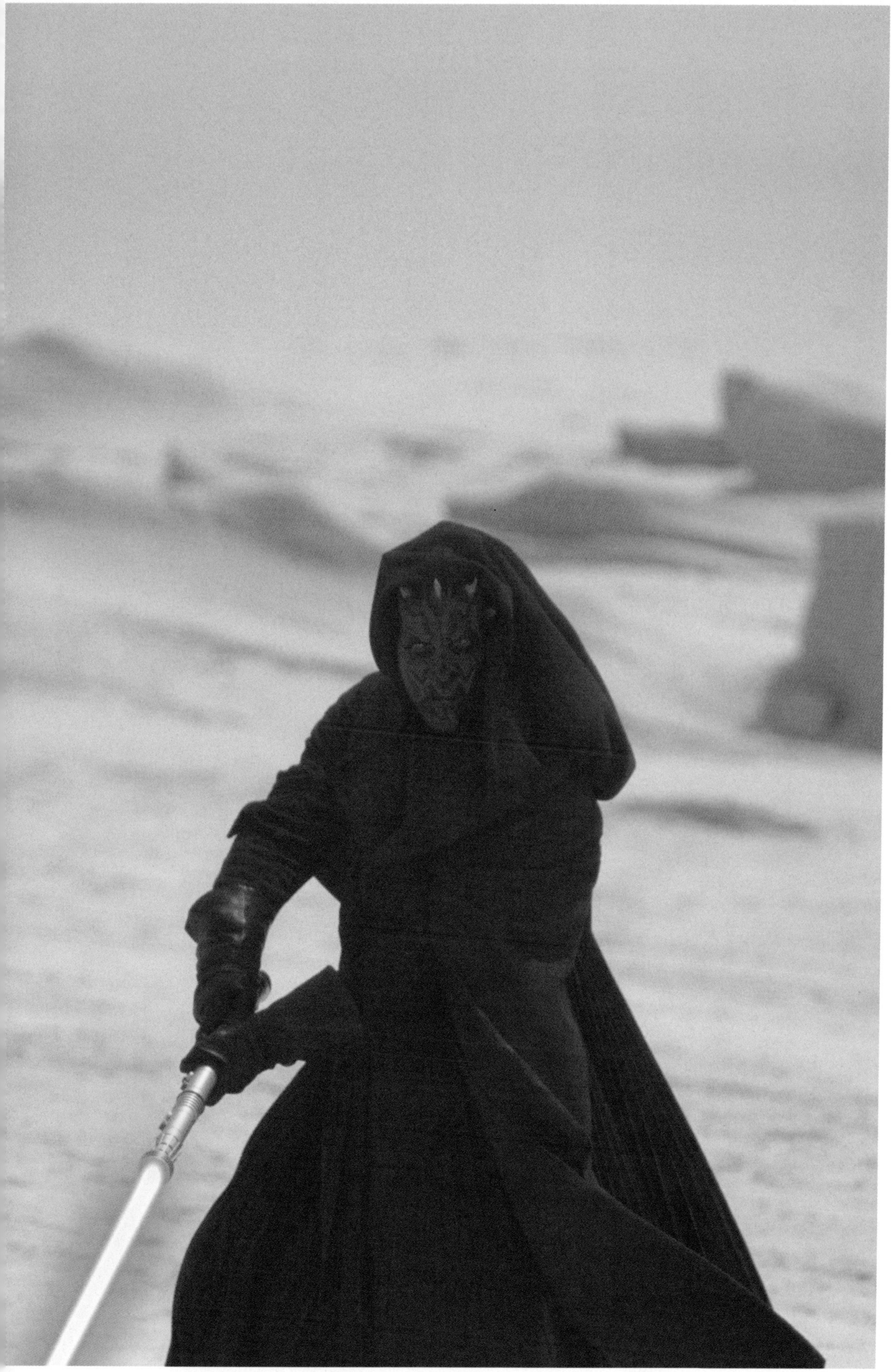

Star Wars: Episode I *The Phantom Menace #3* Photo Variant cover

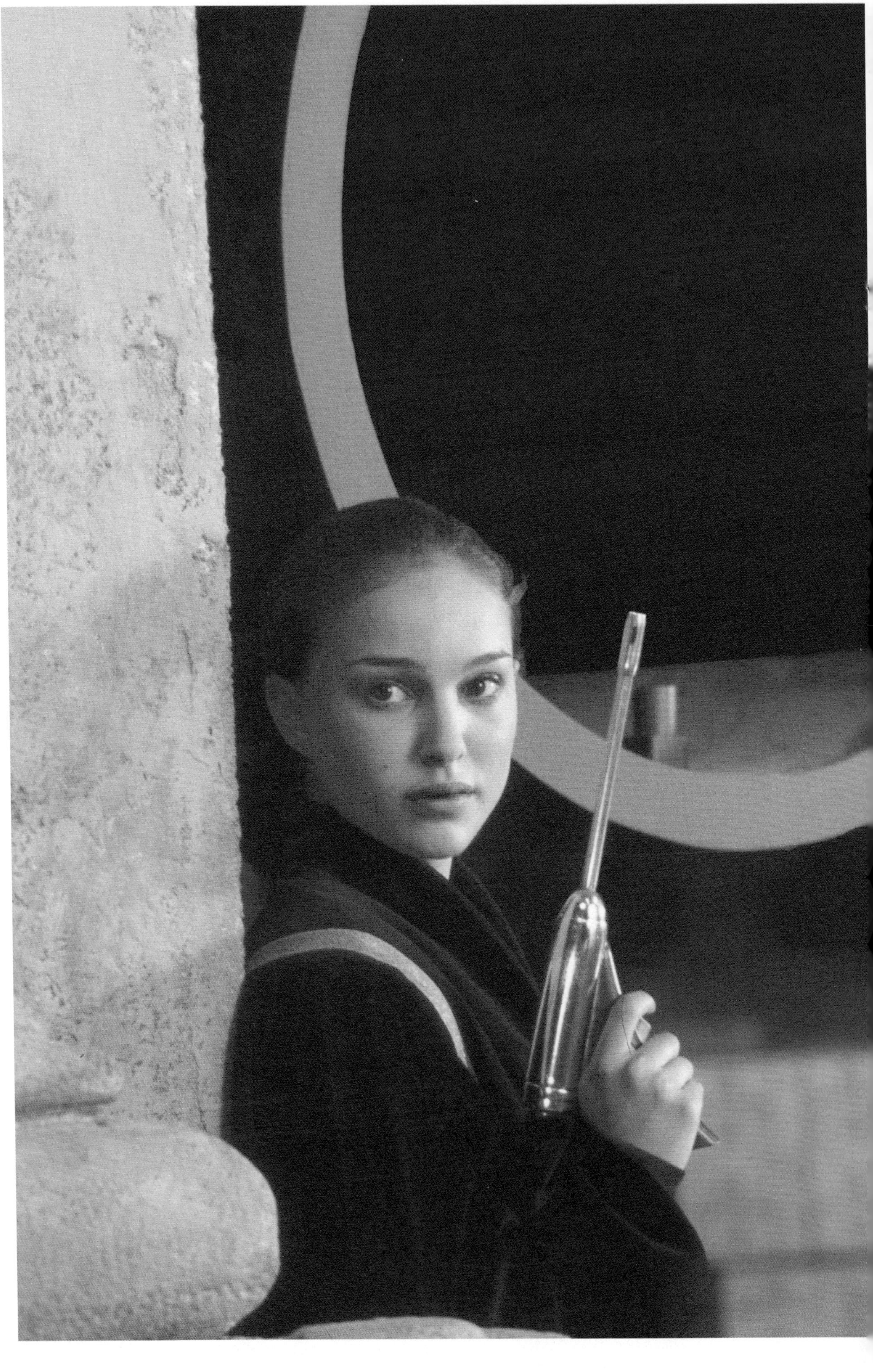

Star Wars: Episode I *The Phantom Menace #4* Photo Variant cover

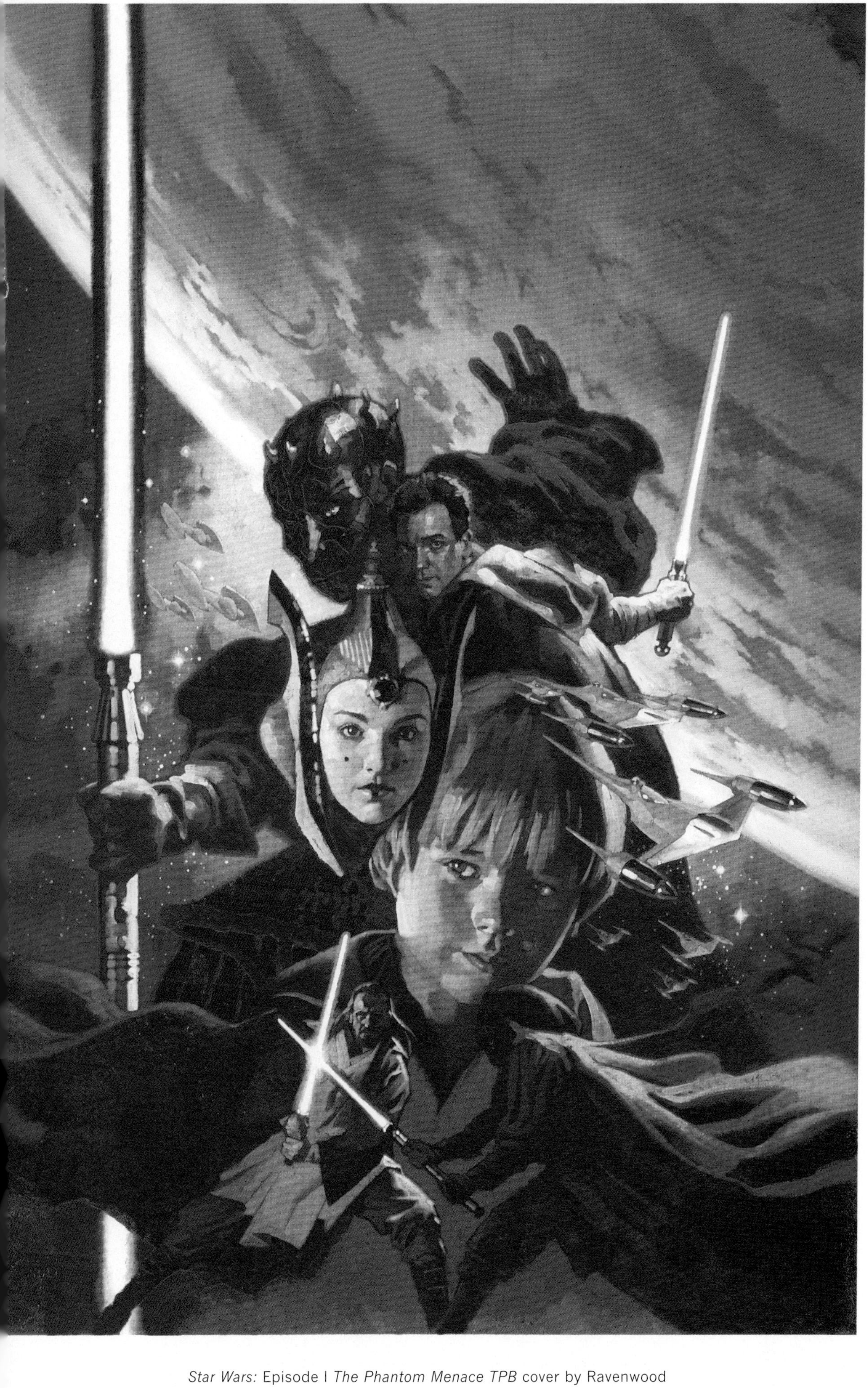

Star Wars: Episode I *The Phantom Menace TPB* cover by Ravenwood

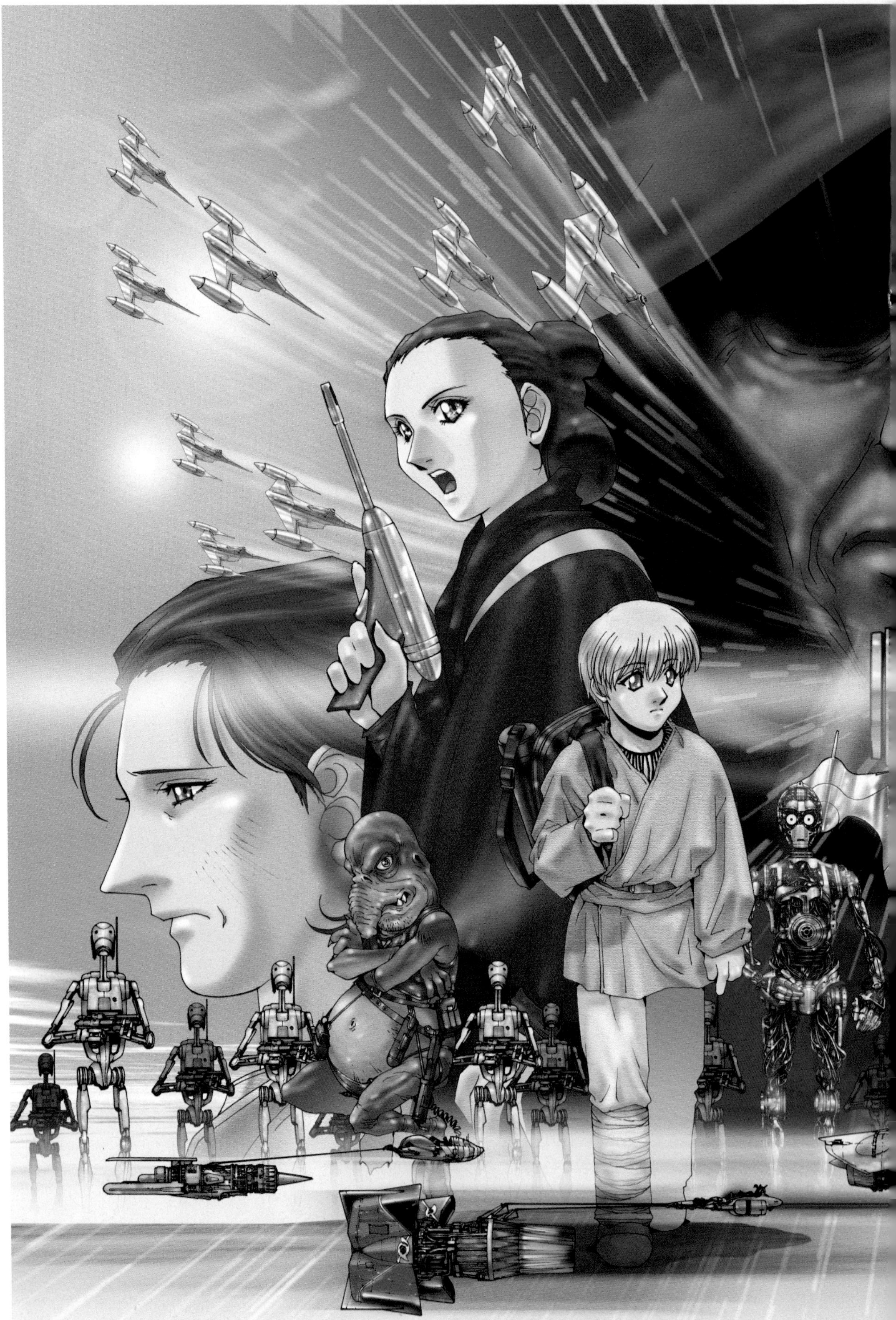

Star Wars: Episode I *The Phantom Menace Manga #1-2* covers by Kia Asamiya

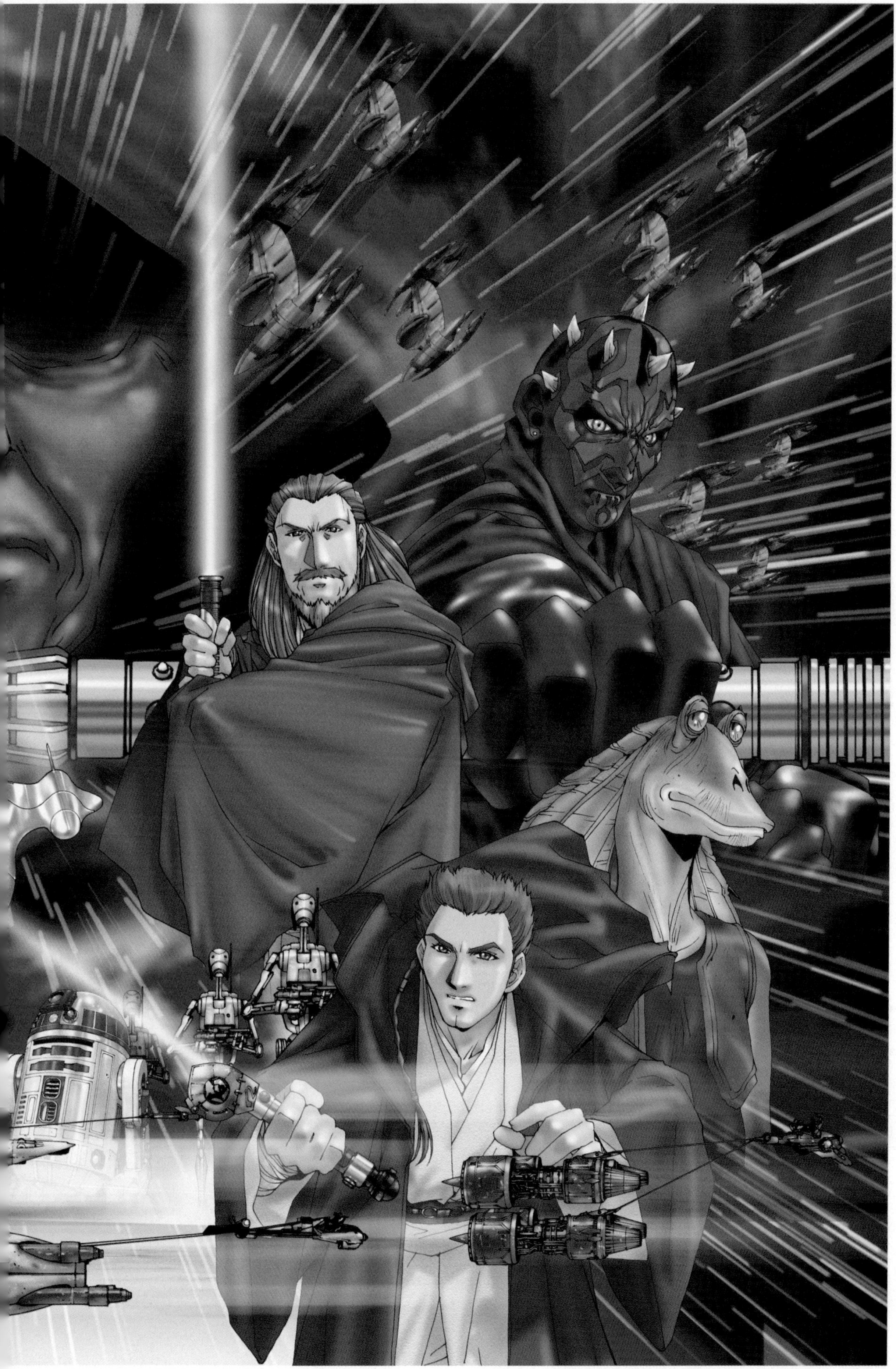

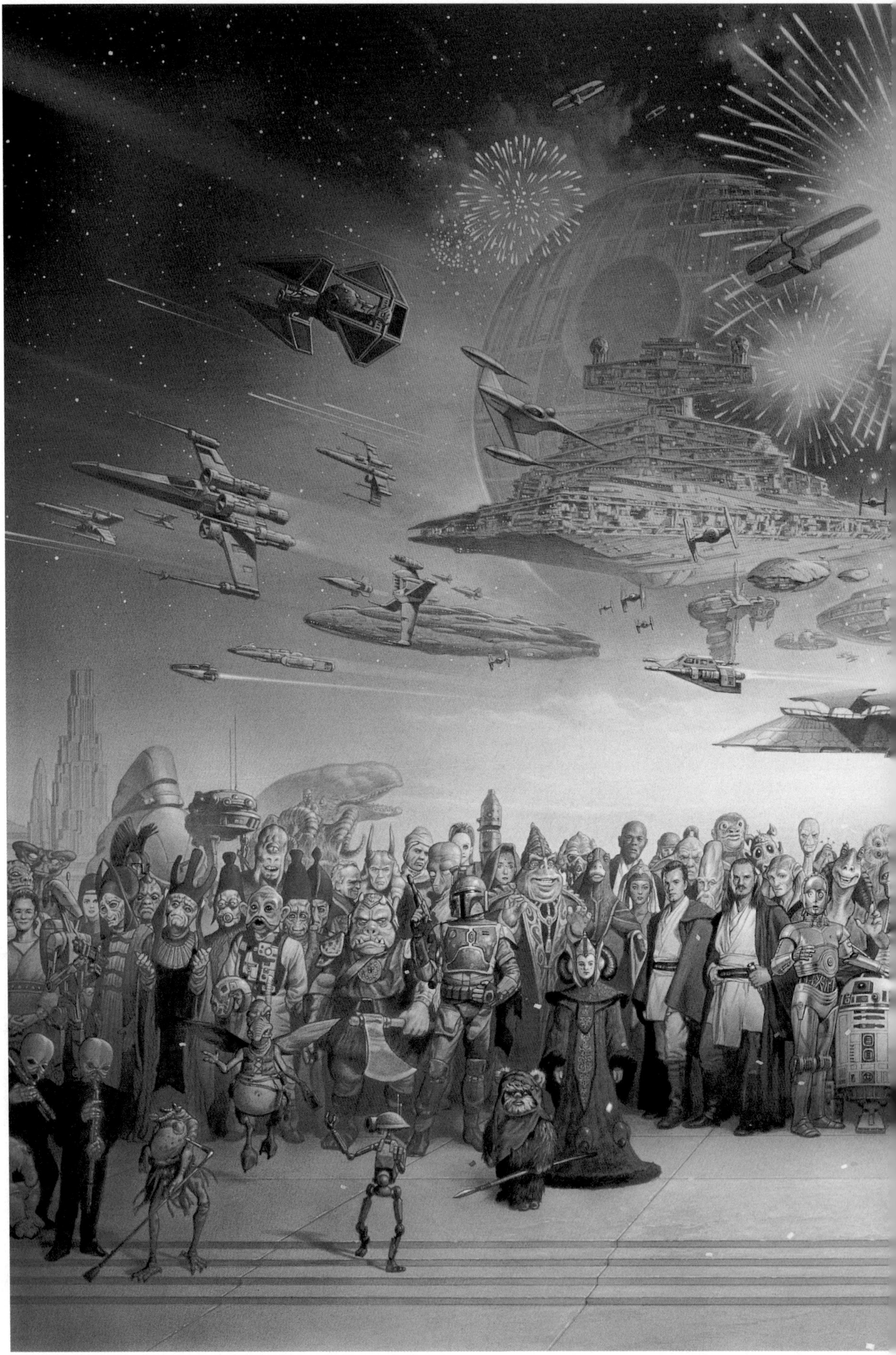

Star Wars Omnibus: The Complete Saga — Episodes I-VI cover by Tsuneo Sanda

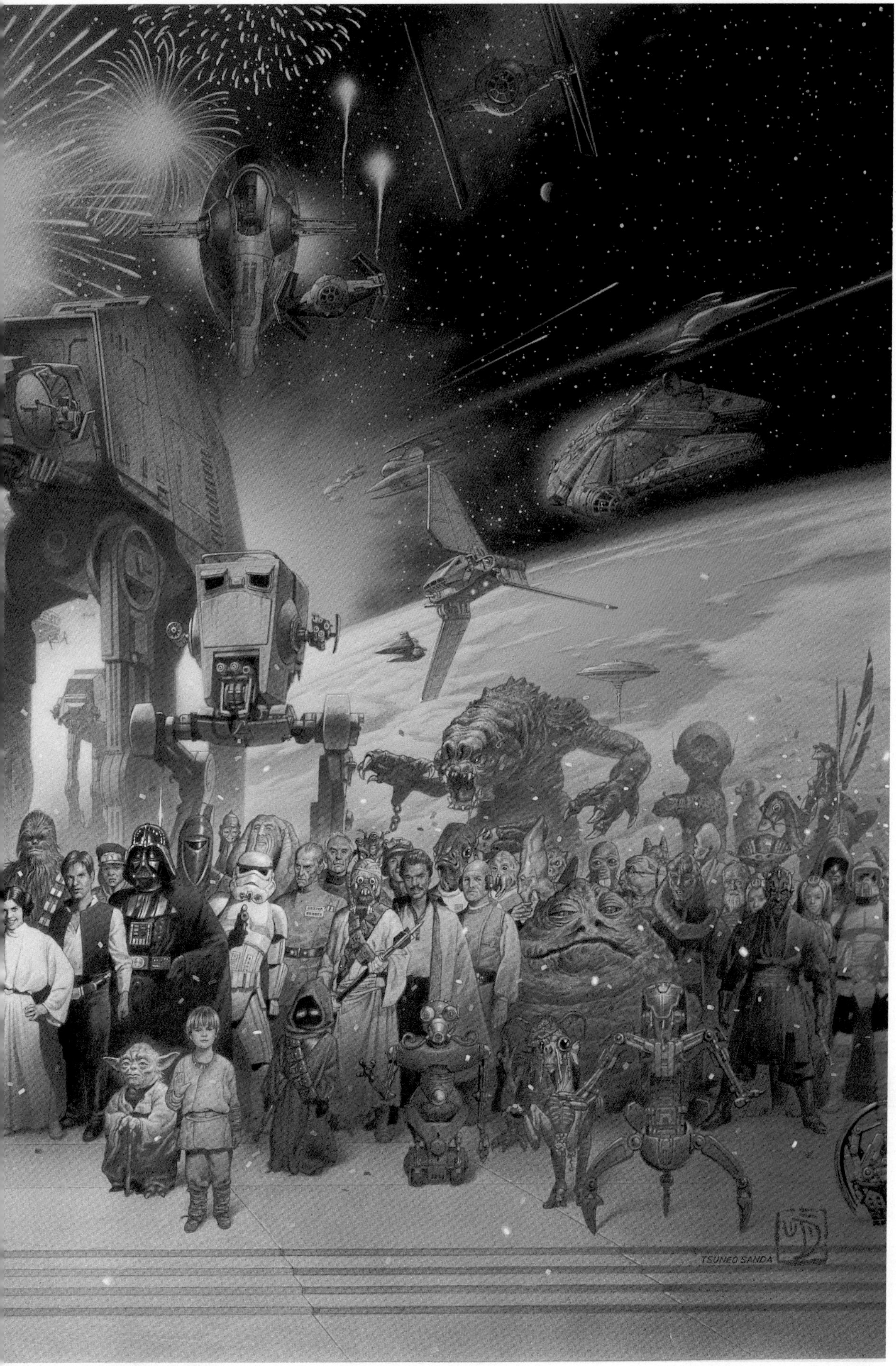
TSUNEO SANDA

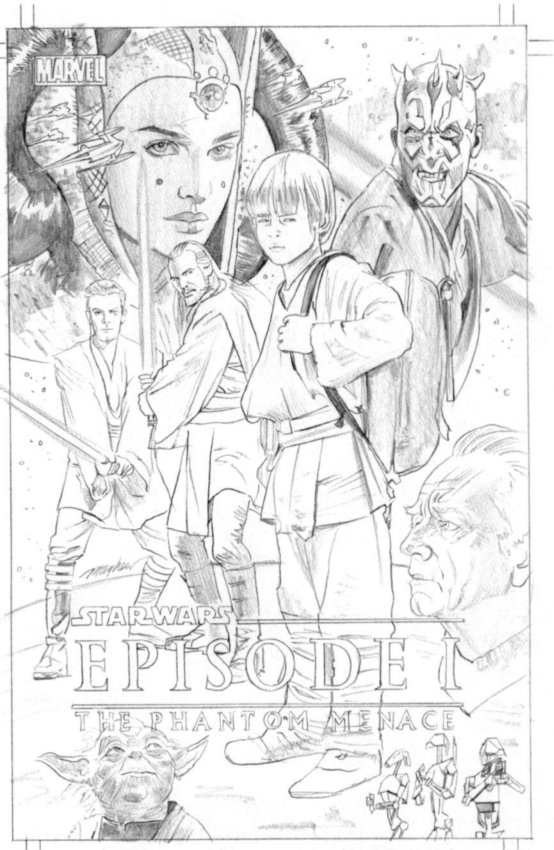
MARVEL
STAR WARS
EPISODE I
THE PHANTOM MENACE

Mayhew

STAR WARS EPISODE 1
HARDCOVER COVER SKETCH A

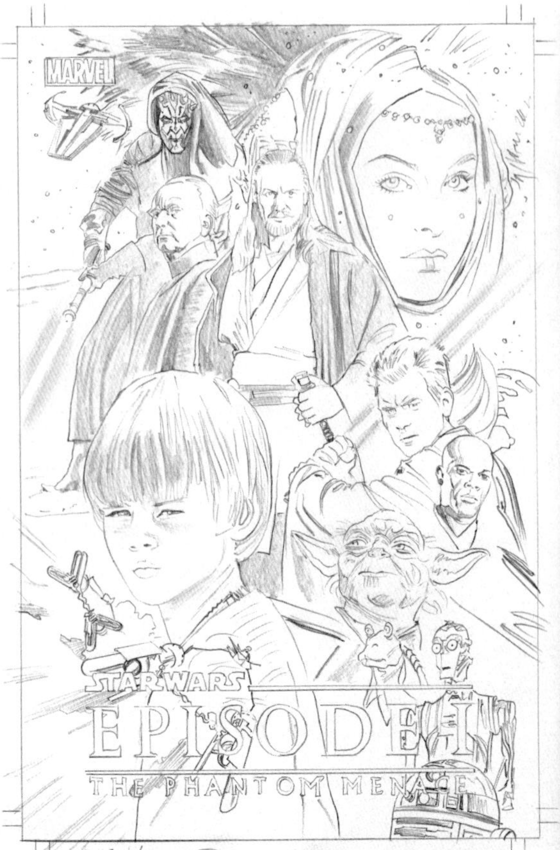
MARVEL
STAR WARS
EPISODE I
THE PHANTOM MENACE

Mayhew

STAR WARS: EPISODE I
HARDCOVER COVER SKETCH 2

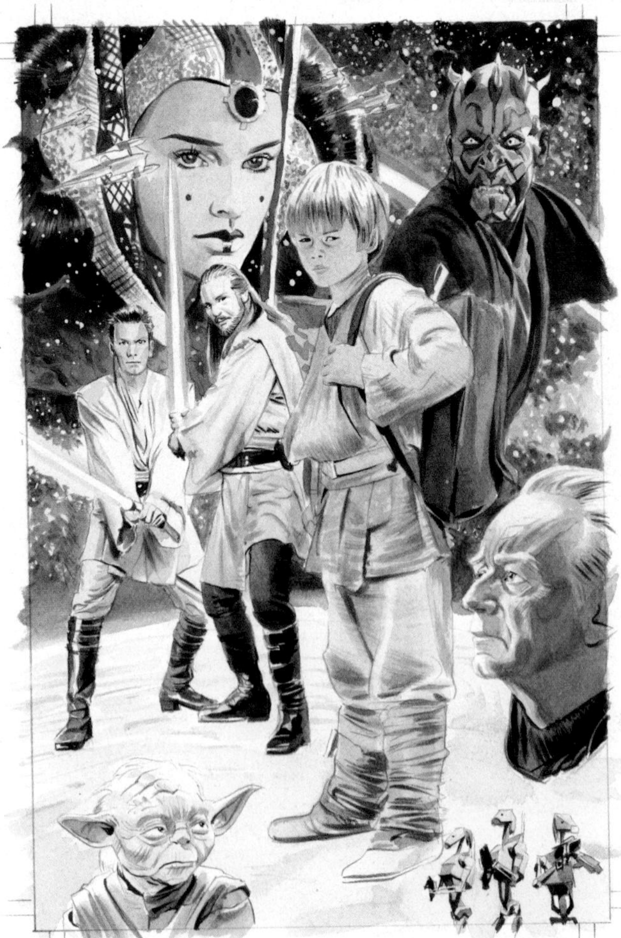

Mayhew

STAR WARS: EPISODE I
HARDCOVER COVER COLOR PRELIM

Star Wars: Episode I *The Phantom Menace HC* cover process by Mike Mayhew

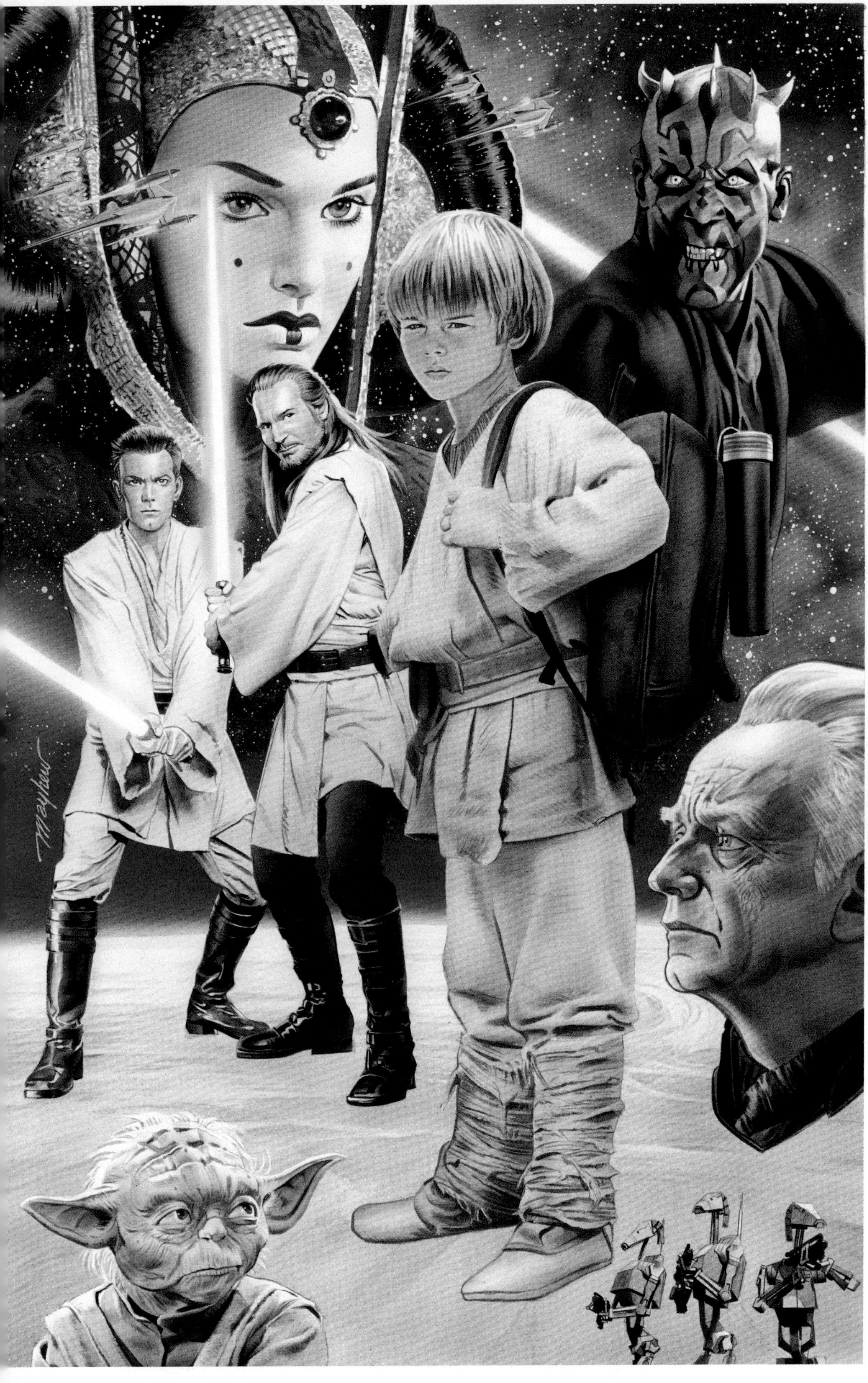

Star Wars: Episode I *The Phantom Menace HC* cover by Mike Mayhew

The story continues in...

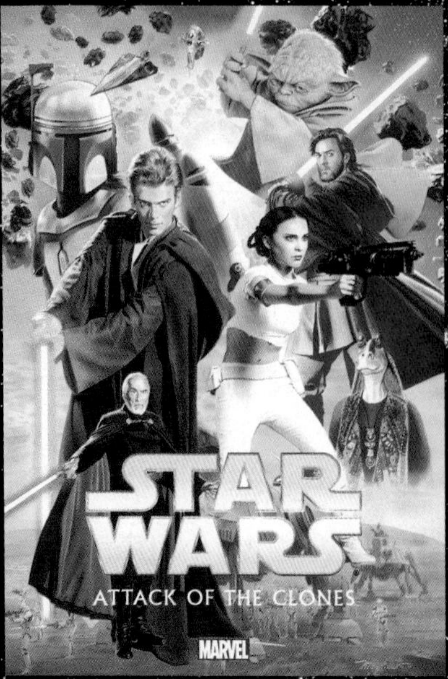
MARVEL
STAR WARS
ATTACK OF THE CLONES

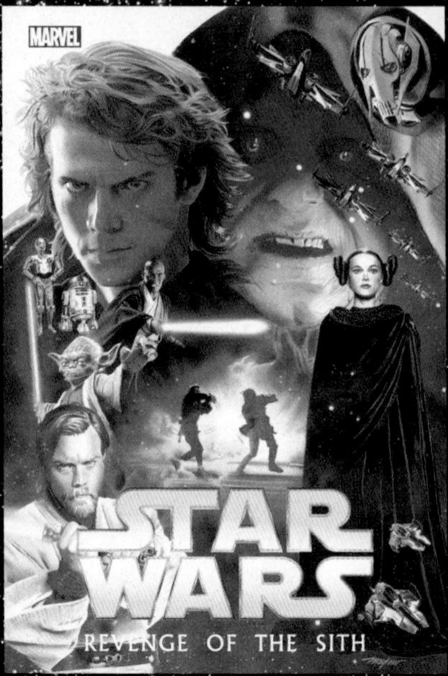
MARVEL
STAR WARS
REVENGE OF THE SITH

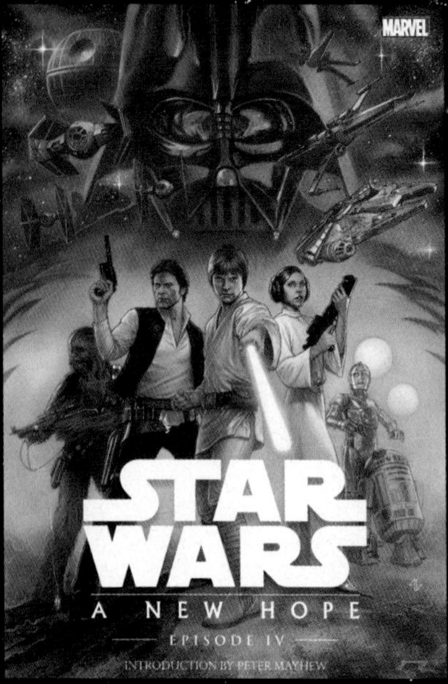
MARVEL
STAR WARS
A NEW HOPE
EPISODE IV
INTRODUCTION BY PETER MAYHEW

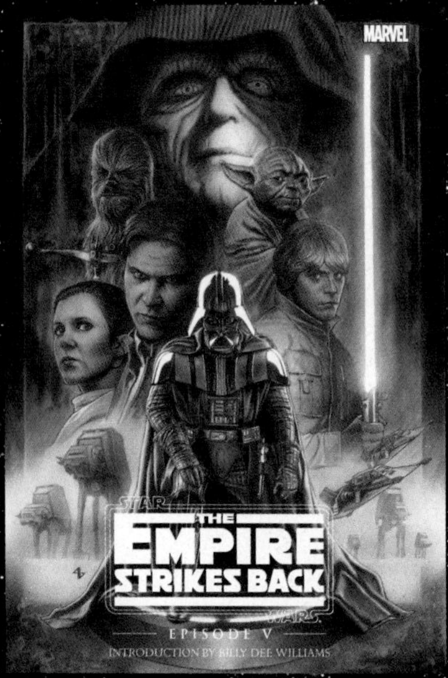
MARVEL
STAR WARS
THE EMPIRE STRIKES BACK
EPISODE V
INTRODUCTION BY BILLY DEE WILLIAMS

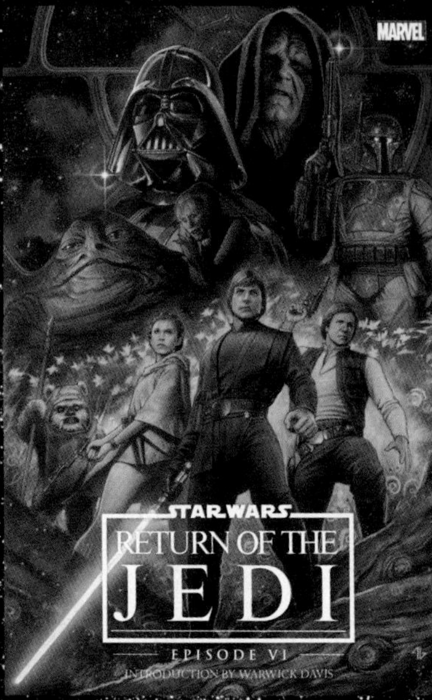
MARVEL
STAR WARS
RETURN OF THE JEDI
EPISODE VI
INTRODUCTION BY WARWICK DAVIS

MARVEL
FREE DIGITAL COPY OFFER
PEEL HERE TO REVEAL CODE

TO REDEEM YOUR CODE FOR A FREE DIGITAL COPY:

1. GO TO MARVEL.COM/REDEEM. OFFER EXPIRES ON 5/25/18.
2. FOLLOW THE ON-SCREEN INSTRUCTIONS TO REDEEM YOUR DIGITAL COPY.
3. LAUNCH THE MARVEL COMICS APP TO READ YOUR COMIC NOW!
4. YOUR DIGITAL COPY WILL BE FOUND UNDER THE *MY COMICS* TAB.
5. READ & ENJOY!

YOUR FREE DIGITAL COPY WILL BE AVAILABLE ON:

MARVEL COMICS APP FOR APPLE® iOS DEVICES

MARVEL COMICS APP FOR ANDROID™ DEVICES

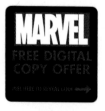